To Sara,

Enjoy many hours of cooking for the Other Family.

love

Jane & Charles

JUNE 2010

Clare & Fiona Ras

Photography: Russel Wasserfall
Design & Illustrations: Roxanne Spears
Food Styling: Joanne Badenhorst
Image Processing: Ray du Toit

JACANA

Sprigs
Entertain

{ Foreword }

THIS book has been a long time coming. Our careers, and therefore our restaurant, have been built in equal part on our passion for food and the joy of feeding groups of friends and family at home or at work. The biggest drive behind Sprigs and our cooking courses is our love of entertaining people. Food really is about entertaining for us, so it made complete sense for us to put together a book that shared some of our favourite menus.

The concept for the book was also driven by our customers at Sprigs. Whether it's a single recipe or an entire menu, cooking for family gatherings or parties is the thing we get asked about all the time. In fact, most of the courses we run in our demo kitchen are about getting people to be more relaxed and creative about feeding people in their homes.

Sprigs Entertain combines some of our favourite dishes with some new recipes we've created using contemporary ingredients. We love to explore different cuisines, and with the raft of exotic ingredients now readily available on supermarket shelves there really is no need to limit your offerings to pasta and pot roast. Of course we have included some crowd-pleasers and old favourites as well as developing menus that will gently push new culinary boundaries for the home cook.

The best way to use this book is to broaden your social circle dramatically. Seriously though, this will probably happen as a matter of course. However, we also hope that you will find some new favourite recipes that will reawaken or encourage the entertainer in you.

The menus are designed to be complete in themselves to make shopping and preparing for an event as easy as possible. Once you have tried a few, you can also mix and match dishes you particularly enjoy with offerings from other menus – our intention, as always, is to guide, not prescribe. Also, within each menu, you might prefer to make more of one dish and leave another out. This is perfect; all the recipes double really well so you can accommodate larger gatherings.

The whole process of putting this book together has been inspiring for us. We dusted off some recipes that we haven't used for a while and combined new ones in ways we hadn't previously considered. In chatting to customers about what should be in there, we were also surprised at how adventurous some people like to be when they cook. It stands to reason, though, as some of our best inspiration comes from suggestions from our customers. We hope that **Sprigs Entertain** becomes a starting point then for your own culinary inspiration and look forward to hearing your feedback and experiences.

Lastly, we think it is worth making the point that entertaining is not hard, nor should it be a chore. If you do it well and stir in a sprinkle of love (and some truffle salt), even scrambled eggs can be the centre of a wonderful gathering. We hope that **Sprigs Entertain** will play a small part in creating some memorable moments in your home.

Clare & Fiona Ras

First published in 2009 by Jacana Media (Pty) Ltd

10 Orange Street, Sunnyside, Auckland Park 2092, South Africa

+27 11 628 3200, www.jacana.co.za

Photography: Russel Wasserfall
Design & Illustrations: Roxanne Spears
Food Styling: Joanne Badenhorst
Image Processing: Ray du Toit

ISBN 978-1-77009-719-3

Printed and bound in Malaysia for Imago

Job no. 000973

See a complete list of Jacana titles at www.jacana.co.za

{ Contents }

{ Morning }

{ Noon }

{ Night }

{ Morning }

{ Morning Menus }

Paris Match

Gone Fishing

A Big Brunch

Great Outdoors

Something Fruity

Tunisian Morning

Paris Match

Boiled Eggs with Asparagus
Soldiers & Olive Salt

Pork Rillette with Sourdough
Melba Toast & Cornichons

Baguette, Cheese Board
& Roasted Grapes

Mango Galettes

Cinnamon & Chocolate Brioche

{ Serves 8 }

Boiled Eggs with Asparagus Soldiers & Olive Salt

PEEL the stalks of the asparagus with a vegetable peeler, and blanch the asparagus for a few minutes in salted, boiling water.

DRAIN. Put the room-temperature eggs in a saucepan, cover generously with water, place on the stove on medium heat, bring to the boil. Set your timer as soon as the water comes to the boil and cook for 4 minutes. As soon as the eggs are cooked, use a slotted spoon to lift them out of the pot and plunge into cold water for 15 seconds, then transfer to egg cups.

SERVE the eggs with the asparagus soldiers and the olive salt on the side.

8 eggs
30ml olive salt
2 bunches asparagus

Pork Rillette with Sourdough Melba Toast & Cornichons

PRE-HEAT the oven to 140°C. Place the pig's trotter and vinegar into a large bowl and cover with boiling water, set aside for 10 minutes. Drain the pig's trotter and rinse under cold running water.

CUBE the pork belly and pork shoulder and transfer to a heavy-based saucepan with a lid that can go in the oven. Pour 900ml of water and add the drained pig's trotter, crushed juniper berries, black pepper, salt, thyme, nutmeg, allspice and halved garlic. Stir the ingredients together, bring the water to the boil, cover with a lid and place in the oven for 4 hours; the pork should be soft and surrounded by liquid fat.

TIP the pork into a sieve placed over a bowl to collect the fat. Remove the thyme stalks and squeeze the garlic into a bowl. Shred the drained meat with 2 forks and add to the soft garlic.

PACK the meat and garlic into a 750ml serving dish, strain the hot fat through a muslin cloth and pour enough liquid onto the pork until the pork is completely covered in liquid. Place in the fridge for a couple of hours or overnight. The pork rillette can last for up to a week in the refrigerator.

SERVE the pork rillete at room temperature with sourdough melbas and cornichons.

Rillette

1 pig's trotter
15ml vinegar
900g pork belly
450g pork shoulder
900ml water
3 juniper berries
2ml ground back pepper
5ml sea salt
4 sprigs thyme
2ml ground nutmeg
2ml ground allspice
1 head garlic

To Serve
sourdough melba toast
1 x jar cornichons

Baguette, Cheese Board & Roasted Grapes

PRE-HEAT the oven to 180°C. Toss the grapes, vinegar, olive oil, salt and pepper together, transfer to a shallow casserole dish and roast for 20 minutes. Transfer to a serving bowl.

SERVE the cheeses at room temperature on a wide breadboard with the roasted grapes and sliced baguette.

CHEESE alternatives: petit grand brie, port salout, a chevin log and Moffin.

125g seedless black grapes
30ml cabernet sauvignon vinegar
30ml olive oil
salt and black pepper
1 x sourdough baguette
1 x wedge Rouy
1 x wedge Caprice des Deux

Mango Galettes

PRE-HEAT the oven to 200°C. Cut the puff pastry into 16 squares and transfer to a greased baking tray. Make a shallow incision (be careful not to cut all the way through) 1cm in from all the sides of pastry squares to form a border, then prick the inside with a fork.

BRUSH the squares with melted butter, then layer the peeled and sliced mango to fit within the borders.

STIR together the brown sugar, vanilla sugar and lemon zest, then scatter over the mango. Bake the mango galettes for 20 minutes or until golden. Cool on a rack.

250g puff pastry
20g melted butter
1 mango
20g dark brown sugar
10g vanilla sugar
zest of half a lemon

Cinnamon & Chocolate Brioche

MAKE the brioche dough a day ahead. Use the paddle attachment on your cake-mixer. Place 110g cake flour, yeast, sugar and salt in the mixing bowl, add the hot water and beat on medium speed for 2 minutes or until smooth.

ADD the eggs one at a time, beating well with each addition. Slowly add the remaining cake flour. Once all the flour has been incorporated, add the softened butter in four stages. Beat for 2 minutes, scrape the dough into a bowl, cover with clingfilm and set aside to prove for 3 hours.

DEFLATE the dough, cover with clingfilm and place the dough in the fridge overnight. The following day, turn the brioche dough out onto a lightly floured work surface. Roll out into a 20 x 30cm rectangle. Brush with the egg glaze, sprinkle the mixture with sugar, cinnamon and chopped chocolate. Fold the dough in half, pressing down gently.

CUT across into 16 strips then, holding the ends, twist each strip to make a spiral shape. Place on a greased baking sheet dusted with flour, cover the dough loosely with clingfilm and set aside for 1 hour, or until doubled in size.

PRE-HEAT the oven to 200°C. Lightly brush the twists with egg wash and bake for 10–15 minutes or until golden. Cool on a rack. To make the icing, whisk the sifted icing sugar, milk and vanilla together and drizzle over the warm cinnamon brioche.

Brioche

500g cake flour
10g dried active yeast
65ml sugar
10ml sea salt
125ml hot water
6 eggs
250g butter

Egg Glaze

1 egg yolk
15ml milk

Cinnamon Brioche

180ml caster sugar
30ml ground cinnamon
100g 65% dark chocolate

Icing

250ml icing sugar
30ml milk
5ml vanilla extract

Gone Fishing

{ Serves 6 }

Tropical Juice

Café Mocha

Cheddar, Paprika & Mushroom Muffins

Carrot, Oat & Pecan Muffins

Scotch Eggs with Pesto

Sirloin Sandwich with
Date, Pear & Red Pepper Chutney

Tropical Juice

IN a blender, blitz the pineapple juice, peeled bananas, honey and lemon juice together until smooth.

POUR the liquid into a flask, add the ice cubes and seal.

600ml pineapple juice
4 ripe bananas
30ml honey
the juice of 1 lemon
250ml ice cubes

Café Mocha

TIP the chopped chocolate, sugar, milk and cream in a saucepan and stir over low heat until melted and smooth. Bring to the boil, whisking constantly with a whisk, then remove from the heat and whisk in the hot coffee.

POUR into a flask. Always use freshly brewed coffee made in a filter pot or an Italian percolator.

200g good quality chocolate (65% cocoa solids)
30ml caster sugar
600ml milk
200ml cream
900ml strong black coffee

Cheddar, Paprika & Mushroom Muffins

HEAT the oil in a frying pan and fry the sliced mushrooms and oregano until tender with no liquid remaining in the pan. Pre-heat the oven to 180°C.

SIFT the flour, baking powder, bicarbonate of soda and salt together into a large mixing bowl. Stir in the cooked mushrooms, grated cheddar, pepper and paprika.

WHISK the honey, egg and yoghurt together, then stir the egg liquid carefully into the flour until just combined. Spoon into a greased muffin tin and bake for 20 minutes or until an inserted skewer comes away clean.

REMOVE the muffins from the tin and cool.

30ml olive oil
100g button mushrooms
2ml dried oregano
250g cake flour
12ml baking powder
2ml bicarbonate of soda
2ml salt
100g cheddar cheese
1ml black pepper
3ml bittersweet paprika
50ml honey
1 egg
200ml natural yoghurt

Carrot, Oat & Pecan Muffins

SOAK the raisins in boiling water for 10 minutes, drain and set aside. Pre-heat the oven to 180°C.

SIFT the flour, baking powder, bicarbonate of soda, salt and cinnamon together in a mixing bowl. Add the oats, chopped walnuts, grated carrots and drained raisins. Whisk the eggs, brown sugar, sunflower oil and vanilla extract. Stir the egg liquid into the flour carefully until just combined.

SPOON into a greased muffin tin and bake for 20 minutes or until an inserted skewer comes away clean. Remove the muffins from the tin and cool.

120g raisins
210g cake flour
3ml baking powder
5ml bicarbonate of soda
2ml salt
5ml ground cinnamon
170g oats
80g walnuts
3 carrots
2 eggs
130g brown sugar
90ml sunflower oil
5ml vanilla extract

Scotch Eggs with Pesto

IN a mixing bowl, combine the sausage meat, paprika, cumin, nutmeg, salt and pepper.

MIX together well and taste for seasoning. Divide the mixture into 12 balls. Pat down each ball on a floured surface to form an oblong shape wide enough to cover an egg. Spread 5ml of pesto on the base, then place one egg across the centre of each oblong of meat and carefully mould the meat around the eggs, making sure there are no cracks.

PLACE 3 shallow bowls on the table, one containing the flour seasoned with salt and pepper, one containing the egg lightly beaten and one containing the breadcrumbs. Dust the sausage-covered eggs in the seasoned flour, then dip one at a time in the beaten egg, coat in the breadcrumbs and set aside on a dinner plate. Place in the fridge for 30 minutes to set.

HEAT the oil in a large saucepan and fry the eggs until golden and cooked through, about 5 minutes. Finally, place on kitchen paper to drain and cool.

PLACE the cooled eggs in a Tiffin box or Tupperware.

2 x 375g pork sausage
5ml paprika
10ml ground cumin
2ml freshly grated nutmeg
12 hard-boiled small eggs
salt and black pepper
60ml homemade pesto
30ml flour
1 egg
100g fresh breadcrumbs
1L sunflower oil for frying

{ makes 12 }

Sirloin Sandwich

CUT each steak in half width-ways and lightly pound with a rolling pin, to flatten each steak, season with salt, pepper and drizzle with olive oil.

HEAT a grill pan until smoking and quickly seal the steaks on both sides. Remove the steaks from the heat and set aside. You may need to grill the steak in batches.

CUT the baguette in half, lengthwise, and drizzle with a little olive oil on the one half and spread a good layer of date and pear chutney on the other half. Season with salt and pepper, lay the grilled sirloin on the base of the baguette, top with half the cheese and rocket and season with salt and pepper. Close the baguette, cut in half and wrap in greaseproof paper. Repeat the process with the other baguette. One baguette will feed 2 people as a sandwich.

3 x 200g sirloin steaks
2 x baguettes
olive oil
salt and black pepper
date and pear chutney
12 slices of mature cheddar
250g rocket

Date, Pear & Red Pepper Chutney

PLACE the cored, chopped pears, pitted dates, brown sugar, vinegar, cinnamon stick, coriander, cumin, sliced onions, sliced peppers and salt in a wide saucepan.

BRING to the boil. Cook on medium heat for 45 minutes or until thick. Be careful to watch the chutney as the dates will start to stick towards the end of cooking.

DECANT into sterilized jars, seal and store.

1kg ripe pears
300g dates
500g brown sugar
340ml vinegar
1 cinnamon stick
20ml ground coriander
20ml ground cumin
500g onions
2 red peppers
10ml salt

{ makes 2 x 400ml jars }

A Big Brunch

Pineapple & Ginger Punch

Wet Oats with Yoghurt,
Plums, Dried Fruit & Nuts

Potted Smoked Fish with
Sourdough Bread

Mild Chilli Tomato Sauce

Sausage & Mushroom
Bread Pudding

Honey, Raisin & Almond Cake

{ Serves 8 }

Pineapple & Ginger Punch

ADD chopped mint leaves, grated ginger and lemon zest to the pineapple juice and allow to steep for 2 hours. When you are ready to serve, combine with the ginger ale and sparkling water and pour over plenty of ice.

750ml pineapple juice
10g mint
5cm knob ginger
zest of 1 lemon
500ml ginger ale
500ml sparkling water

Fruity Wet Oats with Yoghurt

START the night before. Stir the oats, brown rice flakes, chopped apricots, chopped apple rings, raisins, almonds, pumpkin seeds, yoghurt and milk together and place in the fridge overnight.

IN the morning, stir the wet oats and transfer to a serving dish. Top with the sliced plums, dried cranberries and a drizzle of honey.

TRY using different dried fruit and nuts, or serve with a seasonal fruit salad. We like peaches, banana, berries and mango.

200g fine oats
100g brown rice flakes
100g dried apricots
100g dried apple rings
50g raisins
50g whole almonds
50g pumpkin seeds
500g natural yoghurt
80ml milk
6 plums
dried cranberries
30ml honey

Potted Smoked Fish with Sourdough Bread

FLAKE the smoked fish, discarding the skin. Mix together with the mayonnaise, lemon zest and juice, snipped chives, chopped spring onion, crushed Maldon salt and pepper. Check the seasoning and stir in the softened butter. Be careful not to overmix as you still want some texture.

SPOON into 8 ramekins or a shallow serving dish and set in the fridge for a couple of hours. Serve with toasted sourdough bread or crusty white bread.

250g smoked mackerel
120g smoked trout
120ml homemade mayonnaise
zest & juice of 2 lemons
5g chives
small bunch spring onions
10ml Maldon salt
black pepper
110g butter
1 loaf sourdough bread

Mild Chilli Tomato Sauce

GENTLY heat the olive oil, crushed garlic and chilli together until the garlic starts to caramelise; add the tin of tomatoes, chopped coriander, honey, salt and pepper. Bring the sauce to the boil and simmer for 15 minutes.

PURÉE the sauce in a blender. Serve warm.

60ml olive oil
2 garlic cloves
2ml crushed dried chilli
400g tin chopped tomatoes
5g coriander
15ml honey
salt and black pepper

Sausage & Mushroom Bread Pudding

YOU need to assemble the pudding the night before. Grease a 30 x 20cm casserole dish with butter. Remove the skin from the sausages and fry the meat for a couple of minutes, until browned on all sides, then set aside.

FRY the chopped onion and sliced mushroom in olive oil until all the juices have evaporated, and add to the sausage meat. Mix the onion and sausage mixture with the snipped chives, half the feta cheese, half the cheddar cheese, salt and pepper.

SCATTER half the sliced bread on the base of the greased dish, tip in the sausage-meat filling, top with the remaining slices of bread, sprinkle over the rest of the feta and cheddar cheese and lightly press down the filling. Whisk the milk, eggs, salt and pepper together and pour over the pudding.

COVER with clingfilm and place in the fridge overnight. The following day pre-heat the oven to 180°C. Bake the pudding for 45 minutes or until the egg is just set. Serve with the mild chilli tomato sauce.

600g pork sausages
olive oil
250g button mushrooms
1 onion
5g chives
100g crumbled feta
300g grated cheddar
salt and black pepper
1 baguette
625ml milk
5 eggs

Honey, Raisin & Almond Cake

PRE-HEAT the oven to 180°C. Line the base of a 26cm spring-form cake tin with greaseproof paper. Lightly grease with butter and dust with flour. Barely cover the raisins with boiling water and leave to soak for 10 minutes.

MELT the butter, brown sugar and honey over low heat. Remove from the heat and cool for 10 minutes, then stir in the beaten eggs and fold in the sifted flour and drained raisins.

SCRAPE into the prepared cake tin, scatter over the almonds and dot with butter; bake for 45–60 minutes or until an inserted skewer comes away clean. Cool in the tin for 10 minutes.

PLACE the cake on a plate and serve with a wedge of mature cheddar cheese.

100g raisins
160g butter
150g brown sugar
220g honey
3 eggs
300g self-raising flour
100g flaked almonds
100g butter
1 block mature cheddar cheese

Great Outdoors

{ **Serves 8** }

Homemade Chai Tea

Devilled Lamb's Kidneys

Fried Eggs Sprinkled with
Parmesan Cheese

Pot Bread

Caramalised Onions

Salcisse with Salsa Verde

Homemade Chai Tea

DRY-FRY the broken cinnamon stick, and grind to a powder. Repeat with the cloves, peppercorns, crushed cardamom pods and grind to a powder. Mix together the cinnamon and the ground spices and keep in a sealed jar until ready to use.

HEAT the milk, ground spices, sliced ginger, water and caster sugar together and bring to the boil. Remove the saucepan from the heat and set aside for 20 minutes. Return the saucepan to the heat with the tea bags, bring to a simmer, remove from the heat and set aside for a couple of minutes.

REMOVE the tea bags and ladle the hot chai into mugs and serve. If you have any left-over chai, add ice and you'll have iced chai.

3 cinnamon sticks
12 whole cloves
8 black peppercorns
10 green cardamom pods
2 x 5cm knobs ginger
900ml full cream milk
600ml water
120ml caster sugar
4 tea bags

Devilled Lamb's Kidneys

SKIN, halve and core the kidneys and set aside. Lightly whisk the salt, paprika, Worcestershire sauce, lemon juice, Dijon mustard and chicken stock together.

HEAT oil in a frying pan and fry the chopped onion until soft, add the cleaned lamb kidneys and seal on both sides. Pour in the paprika liquid and cook for 5–10 minutes or until the sauce has reduced and thickened.

GARNISH with chopped parsley and serve with the Parmesan fried eggs.

16 lamb kidneys
5ml salt
3ml paprika
10ml Worcestershire sauce
juice of half a lemon
5ml Dijon mustard
250ml chicken stock
60ml sunflower oil
half an onion
2 sprigs parsley

Fried Eggs Sprinkled with Parmesan Cheese

HEAT the oil and butter in a cast-iron frying pan until just starting to foam, pour in the cracked eggs, season with salt and pepper, cover with a lid and cook for one minute. Remove the lid and continue to cook the eggs to your liking.

SPRINKLE with grated Parmesan cheese and serve.

30ml sunflower oil
30ml butter
8 eggs
salt and black pepper
60g Parmesan cheese

Pot Bread

GREASE a number 3 flat-bottomed cast-iron pot with oil and heat on the fire while you are mixing the bread.

IN a mixing bowl, stir the flour, salt, grated cheese and chopped parsley together, then stir in the beer and milk and mix until the dough comes together to form a ball.

PLACE the dough in the heated pot, cover with the lid and move the pot to a cooler section of your fire, cover the lid, top with a few hot coals and cook for approximately 45 minutes, keeping an eye on the heat of your coals on the bottom and top of the bread.

TO test that the bread is done, tap the base of the loaf; the base should sound hollow when tapped with your finger.

15ml sunflower oil
500g self-raising flour
5ml salt
100g cheddar cheese
10g Italian parsley
340ml beer
100ml milk

Caramalised Onions

HEAT the olive oil and butter in a cast-iron frying pan and fry the sliced red onion until soft. Add the sliced garlic, thyme leaves, salt, pepper and balsamic reduction.

BRING the onions to the boil and cook for 20–30 minutes until thick.

60ml olive oil
60ml butter
6 red onions
2 garlic cloves
2 sprigs thyme leaves
salt and black pepper
30ml balsamic reduction

Salcisse with Salsa Verde

BRAAI the sausages until cooked to your liking.

FOR the salsa verde, roughly chop the parsley leaves, basil leaves, mint leaves and peeled garlic together to a coarse texture, then tip into a bowl.

ROUGHLY chop the anchovies and capers, then add to the bowl with the herbs, pour in the red wine vinegar and olive oil, stirring constantly, then season with the Dijon mustard, salt and pepper.

8 salcisse sausages

Salsa Verde

50g Italian parsley
50g basil
20g mint
3 garlic cloves
6 anchovy fillets
30ml capers
30ml red wine vinegar
75ml olive oil
15ml Dijon mustard
salt and black pepper

Something Fruity

Almond Lemon Scones

Fruit Salad with Lemongrass & Mint

Muesli with Raisins & Toasted
Pecan Nuts

Blueberry Muffins

Beetroot, Carrot, Grape & Ginger Juice

Plum & Custard Tartlets

Almond Lemon Scones

PRE-HEAT the oven to 180°C. Sift the flour and baking powder into a large mixing bowl and rub in the butter until the mixture resembles fine breadcrumbs. Stir in the sugar, almond extract and chopped almonds and pour in the milk.

STIR or 'cut' the mixture with a knife to bring the dough together. Transfer to the work surface and lightly roll out with a rolling pin to about 30 x 30cm in length and 4cm thick.

CUT out the scones with a round pastry cutter, lay on a greased baking sheet, brush each scone with a little milk and bake for 12–15 minutes.

COOL on a wire rack. Serve with butter and your favourite jam. Cherry goes particularly well with these scones.

450g cake flour
15ml baking powder
75g butter
50g brown sugar
10ml almond extract
50g whole almonds
300ml milk
butter to serve
jar cherry jam

{ makes 10 scones }

Fresh Fruit Salad
with Lemongrass & Mint

FOR the lemongrass syrup, pour the water into a saucepan and add the sugar, bruised and roughly chopped lemongrass and mint. Bring to the boil and simmer for 5 minutes. Remove the saucepan from the heat and set aside for 30 minutes.

STRAIN the syrup, then chill in the fridge until needed. Pour half of the syrup into a bowl, stir together with the peeled and chopped mango, segmented oranges, cored and chopped apples, hulled strawberries, sliced banana and mint leaves.

SPOON the fruit salad into bowls, top with yoghurt, honey and serve with Homemade Muesli with Raisins and Toasted Pecan Nuts and a jug with the rest of the syrup.

Lemongrass & Mint Syrup

250ml water
125ml sugar
3 lemongrass sticks
5 sprigs mint

Salad

1 ripe mango
2 oranges
2 apples
200g strawberries
2 bananas
2 sprigs mint
300ml Greek yoghurt
100ml honey

Muesli with Raisins & Toasted Pecan Nuts

PRE-HEAT the oven to 170°C. In a large mixing bowl, stir the oats, sunflower seeds, wheat germ, coconut, sugar and sesame seeds together.

WHISK together the water, oil, salt and vanilla. Stir the water liquid into the oats, press into shallow baking trays and bake for 20–30 minutes, turning occasionally. The muesli will be golden in colour.

COOL the tray on a wire rack and stir in the raisins and toasted pecan nuts. Once cooled completely, store in an airtight container. Try varying the dried fruit and nuts to your taste.

500g fine oats
70g sunflower seeds
140g wheat germ
100g desiccated coconut
140g brown sugar
40g sesame seeds
200ml water
200ml sunflower oil
3ml salt
5ml vanilla essence
100g raisins
100g pecan nuts

Blueberry Muffins

PRE-HEAT the oven to 180°C. For the topping, crumble the chopped butter, brown sugar and cake flour together and set aside.

FOR the muffins, cream the butter and sugar until light and fluffy, then slowly beat in the eggs one at a time. Sift the flour, baking powder and cinnamon over the butter mixture, stir in the lemon zest and the blueberries.

SPOON into a greased muffin tin, sprinkle over the topping and bake for 20 minutes or until an inserted skewer comes away clean. Remove the muffins from the tin and cool.

Topping

60g butter
60g brown sugar
60g cake flour

Muffins

120g butter
225g caster sugar
2 eggs
280g cake flour
12ml baking powder
5ml ground cinnamon
100ml natural yoghurt
zest of 1 lemon
125g blueberries

{ makes 12 small muffins }

Beetroot, Carrot, Grape & Ginger Juice

TRIM, roughly chop the beetroot, carrot and peeled ginger, then process them with the grapes and mint leaves in a juice extractor. We like to serve the juice as is, but it is great poured over ice.

8 beetroots
4 carrots
5cm knob ginger
250g seedless green grapes
4 sprigs mint

Plum & Custard Tartlets

FOR the custard, heat the milk and vanilla in a medium sauce-pan and gently bring to the boil. Remove from the heat and set aside for 5 minutes to allow the flavours to infuse.

WHISK the eggs, egg yolks and 30g of caster sugar for 5 minutes. Stir in the flour and corn flour and beat until the mix is lump-free. Whisk the warm milk into the eggs and pour the liquid back into the saucepan.

SIMMER over medium heat until thick, stirring continuously with a wooden spoon. Scrape into a bowl and sprinkle over 10ml caster sugar to prevent a skin forming, then allow to cool. The custard can be made the day before.

PRE-HEAT the oven to 200°C. Roll out the puff pastry on a lightly floured surface until 3mm thick, cut discs with a round cutter 9cm in diameter. Grease and flour one 12-muffin tin and place a disc in each. Spoon the custard into the pastry cases, top with the stoned and halved plums, skin side down.

BAKE for 20–30 minutes. Cool in the tin for 10 minutes before removing the tarts and brush with apricot jam.

Custard
250ml milk
2ml vanilla bean paste
3 eggs
3 egg yolks
50g caster sugar
15g cake flour
10g corn flour
10ml caster sugar

Tarts
250g puff pastry
6 plums
30ml smooth apricot jam

{ **12 muffin size tartlets** }

Tunisian
Morning

Boiled Eggs with Paprika Dukkah

Crunchy Vegetables with Ricotta Dip

Pita Breads

Chopped Olive Salad

Roasted Red Pepper Hummus

Fresh Fruit with Orange Blossom
Syrup & Cinnamon Labne

Boiled Eggs with Paprika Dukkah

PRE-HEAT the oven to 180°C. Toast the sesame seeds in an ovenproof dish for about 5–8 minutes or until golden. Toast the hazelnuts in a shallow ovenproof dish for 12 minutes; the skins should burst open and the nuts should be lightly coloured. Turn the nuts into a clean dishcloth, bundle up and rub them vigorously to release their outer skins. Toast the coriander and cumin seeds in a dry frying pan, about 4 minutes.

TIP the sesame and hazelnuts into a food processor and blitz until coarsely ground. Grind the toasted coriander and cumin seeds in a mortar and pestle until finely ground. Stir the ground hazelnuts, ground seeds, salt, pepper and paprika together. Store in a sealed jar until ready to use.

PUT the room-temperature eggs in a saucepan, cover with water, place on the stove and bring to the boil. As soon as the water comes to the boil, set your timer for 6 minutes. As soon as the eggs are cooked, use a slotted spoon to transfer to iced water and leave to cool.

SERVE the eggs with the paprika dukkah on the side. Your friends will need to peel their own eggs and dip them into the paprika dukkah.

8 eggs

Paprika Dukkah

200ml sesame seeds
70ml hazelnuts
70ml coriander seeds
70ml cumin seeds
2ml sea salt
2ml ground black pepper
15ml sweet smoked paprika

Crunchy Vegetables with Ricotta Dip

FOR the ricotta dip, tip the ricotta into a blender with the crushed garlic, lemon zest, milk, salt, pepper, and chopped parsley and blend until smooth. You may need extra milk, as you are looking for spreadable consistency.

SERVE the trimmed vegetables on a platter with a bowl of ricotta dip.

Ricotta Dip

250g ricotta cheese
1 garlic clove
zest of 1 lemon
60ml milk
salt and black pepper
small bunch Italian parsley

Veggies

200g baby cucumbers
1 bunch asparagus
250g cherry tomatoes
1 bunch radish

Pita Breads

SPRINKLE the yeast and sugar in a large bowl and whisk in the water, then stir in the olive oil. Beat in one handful of the flour and the salt until you have a smooth batter. Add the remaining flour, a handful at a time, kneading the dough well each time until all the flour has been incorporated. The dough should become soft and sticky.

TURN the dough out onto a lightly floured work surface and cover with the bowl for 5 minutes. Knead the dough until it becomes smooth and shiny, then place in a lightly greased bowl, cover with clingfilm until it doubles in size, about 45–60 minutes. Deflate the dough on a lightly floured surface and divide into 12 equal pieces, roll each between your hands to form smooth balls, then cover with a damp tea towel.

PRE-HEAT the oven to 220°C with the baking tray in the oven. Roll out each ball of dough to about a 15cm circle, lay the dough rounds on a lightly floured tea towel, and leave to rise for 30 minutes, until doubled in size. Quickly transfer the first batch of pita breads to the hot baking tray and lightly sprinkle with water to keep them pale.

BAKE for 2 minutes without opening the oven door. The pitas should have puffed up. Watch them carefully: they must not brown or become too crispy. Transfer the cooked pitas to a rack to cool, then cover with a tea towel and continue to cook the remaining pitas.

10g instant dried yeast
2ml sugar
280ml lukewarm water
15ml olive oil
450g stoneground flour
5ml sea salt

Chopped Olive Salad

PIT and roughly chop the kalamata and green olives and place in a mixing bowl. Stir in chopped spring onion, chopped mint leaves, olive oil, lemon juice, salt and pepper. Use good quality olives for this dish.

100g kalamata olives
100g green olives
1 bunch spring onion
10g mint
30ml olive oil
juice of half a lemon
salt and black pepper

Roasted Red Pepper Hummus

ROAST the pepper over an open flame until blackened, wrap in clingfilm and set aside for 10 minutes.

PEEL and seed the blackened pepper and tip into a blender. Add the drained chickpeas and olive oil, whiz together until roughly chopped. Add the lemon juice, crushed garlic, tahini, cayenne pepper, salt and pepper and whiz again until smooth. Check the seasoning. If the hummus is too thick, loosen with a little water.

SCRAPE onto a platter and set aside. When you are ready to serve, drizzle with extra olive oil.

1 red pepper
400g tin chickpeas
70ml olive oil
juice of half a lemon
1 garlic clove
90ml tahini
pinch of cayenne pepper
salt and black pepper

Fresh Fruit with Orange Blossom Syrup & Cinnamon Labne

FOR the labne, whisk together the caster sugar and cinnamon to the yoghurt, put into a sieve lined with muslin and set it over a bowl. Let the yoghurt drain for 24 hours, giving it a little help every so often by picking up the bag and squeezing it.

TO make the syrup, gently heat the honey, orange juice and orange flower water together in a small saucepan. Once the honey has melted, boil for one minute. Set aside to cool.

SCATTER the peeled and sliced mangoes onto a platter with the hulled strawberries.

PEEL the cheesecloth from around the labne and dollop onto the sliced mango and spoon over the syrup; scatter over toasted and chopped pistachio nuts

Cinnamon Labneh
60ml caster sugar
5ml ground cinnamon
400g Greek yoghurt

Syrup
100ml honey
60ml orange juice
30ml orange flower water

Serving
4 ripe mangoes
250g strawberries
25g pistachios

{ Noon }

{ Noon Menus }

Long Italian Lunch

A Mediterranean Breeze

Jersey Cookout

Flavours of Spain

Greek Accents

Alfresco Lunch

A Moroccan Twist

Lunch in Lebanon

Thai Island Style

Afternoon Delights

Long Italian Lunch

{ Serves 8 }

Chicken Tonnato

Spaghetti Salad with Fried Eggs & Chilli

Gratin of Mushrooms with Bacon

Boiled Leg of Lamb
with Beans & Caper Sauce

Crustless Potato & Green Bean Tart

Green Salad with a Dijon Vinaigrette

Flourless Chocolate Tart
with Poached Pears

Chicken Tonnato

PRE-HEAT the oven to 180°C. Heat the olive oil in a frying pan that can go in the oven and brown the seasoned chicken breasts on both sides, starting on the skin side. Turn the chicken breasts skin side up, and roast in the oven for 20–30 minutes or until cooked through. Remove the chicken and set aside.

HEAT the remaining olive oil in the frying pan and fry the finely chopped carrot, finely chopped celery, finely chopped onion and crushed garlic. Fry for a couple of minutes without colouring. Pour in the white wine, chopped sage, chopped rosemary and drained tuna. Bring the wine to the boil and simmer for 10 minutes, then let the tuna mixture cool. Purée the tuna mixture until smooth, stir in the mayonnaise, lemon juice, salt and pepper.

SLICE the chicken and arrange over the shredded fresh spinach, top with the tuna sauce and garnish with anchovy fillets. (You could also wilt the spinach with a little olive oil in a pan if you don't fancy fresh.)

30ml olive oil
8 chicken breasts with skin & bone
salt and black pepper
2 carrots
2 celery stalks
2 onions
2 garlic cloves
500ml dry white wine
6 fresh sage leaves
2 sprigs fresh rosemary
150g tuna packed in oil
250ml mayonnaise
juice of 1 lemon
200g baby spinach
8 anchovy fillets

Spaghetti Salad with Fried Eggs & Chilli

COOK the pasta in salted boiling water until dente.

HEAT the olive oil and butter in a large frying pan over medium heat. Fry the crushed garlic until just starting to colour, add the eggs and cook, sunny-side up, basting with a spoon, for 2–3 minutes without turning, or until the eggs are just done (the yolks must remain runny). Remove the pan from the heat and sprinkle eggs with salt, pepper and dried chilli. You must time this dish so that the pasta is ready as soon as the eggs are done.

TOSS the drained pasta with olive oil, season with salt, pepper, grated Parmesan and chopped parsley, and tip the pasta on a serving dish. Pour the contents of the egg pan, including the oil, butter and garlic, onto the pasta.

GARNISH with chopped oregano and serve. Pass the additional Parmigiano-Reggiano at the table.

500g spaghetti
45ml olive oil
25g butter
2 garlic cloves
4 eggs
salt and black pepper
2ml crushed dried chilli
50g Parmigiano-Reggiano
50g Italian parsley
4 sprigs oregano

Gratin of Mushrooms with Bacon

PRE-HEAT the oven to 180°C. Grease a shallow baking dish about 23 x 35cm with the olive oil and 15g of the butter. Arrange half the sliced mushrooms over the bottom of the prepared dish, season with salt and pepper, and add half the crushed garlic.

SPRINKLE over half the grated 2 cheeses, and half the chopped bacon, chopped tomatoes, finely chopped onions and chopped parsley. Make another layer of mushrooms, garlic, cheeses, bacon, tomatoes, onion and parsley.

SEASON with salt and pepper. Spread the breadcrumbs on top and dot with the remaining butter. Bake for 30 minutes and serve.

15ml olive oil
100g butter
1 kg mixed mushrooms
(button, black and portobellini)
salt and black pepper
2 garlic cloves
100g Parmesan
100g pecorino
150g streaky bacon
4 tomatoes
2 medium onions
10g Italian parsley
40g fresh white breadcrumbs

Boiled Leg of Lamb
with Beans & Caper Sauce

SOAK the beans in water overnight. Bring a large saucepan, big enough to hold the leg of lamb with water. Season the leg of lamb with salt, pepper and chopped butter, wrap in a dishcloth and tie with string. Tip the leg of lamb into the hot water; add the drained beans, peeled carrots, trimmed leeks, peeled onion, peeled garlic and rosemary sprigs.

BRING to the boil and simmer until the lamb is cooked, allowing 45 minutes per 500g. Drain, reserving 300ml of the lamb stock. Drain the beans and vegetables, chop the vegetables and tip into a bowl with the beans, garlic, salt, pepper and a good glug of olive oil, and keep warm.

FOR the caper sauce, melt the butter, add the flour and whisk until incorporated, add the hot milk, stock, salt, pepper, and stir until thick. Stir in the roughly chopped capers and finely chopped parsley. Tip the beans onto a platter, top with the sliced lamb and serve the caper sauce.

200g small white beans
1.3kg leg of lamb
100g butter
salt and black pepper
2 carrots
2 leeks
2 onions
1 bulb garlic
2 sprigs rosemary
olive oil

Caper sauce
45ml butter
45ml cake flour
300ml milk
300ml lamb stock
60ml small capers
5g Italian parsley

Crustless Potato & Green Bean Tart

PRE-HEAT the oven to 180°C. Boil the potatoes in salted boiling water until tender, drain and pass through a ricer and keep warm. Blanch the green beans in salted water until tender, drain and finely chop.

SOAK 250ml of breadcrumbs in the milk and set aside. Stir together the mash potato, green beans, soaked bread, crushed garlic, chopped oregano, chopped parsley, grated Parmesan, ricotta, beaten eggs, salt and pepper together.

SPOON the mixture into a greased baking tray or spring-form tin, smooth the surface, score the top and scatter over the remaining breadcrumbs. Bake until golden, about 40 minutes.

SERVE warm or at room temperature. Drizzle over a little oregano oil and serve.

450g baking potatoes
salt and black pepper
340g green beans
350ml breadcrumbs
180ml milk
3 garlic cloves
3 sprigs oregano
5g Italian parsley
100g Parmesan cheese
60ml ricotta cheese
4 eggs

Green Salad with a Dijon Vinaigrette

FIRST make the dressing: whisk the sugar, Dijon mustard, vinegar, olive oil, salt and pepper together.

FOR the salad, tip the rocket and salad leaves into a bowl and add the parsley leaves, mint leaves and sliced spring onions.

JUST before serving, toss the leaves with enough dressing to make them glisten.

Dressing

60ml caster sugar
60ml Dijon mustard
60ml red wine vinegar
100ml olive oil
salt and black pepper

Salad

100g rocket
250g mixed salad leaves
20g Italian parsley
20g mint
8 spring onions

Flourless Chocolate Tart with Poached Pears

PRE-HEAT the oven to 180°C. Line the base of a 26cm spring-form cake tin with greaseproof paper. Lightly grease with butter and dust with flour.

MELT the chopped chocolate on top of a double boiler set over simmering water over medium water, then set aside to cool.

TIP the butter into the bowl of a cake mixer and beat until light and fluffy, gradually add the sugar, beating for 2–3 minutes. Add the egg yolks one at a time, beating well between each addition, then add the chocolate, beating just enough to blend it in. Stir in the ground almonds and brandy and set aside.

WHISK the egg whites and salt together until medium-stiff peaks form. Fold one-third into the chocolate mixture, then fold in the rest in 2 more batches, taking care not to deflate the batter. Pour into the prepared cake tin and bake for 45–60 minutes or until an inserted skewer comes away clean.

COOL in the tin for 10 minutes and then remove the sides of the spring-form tin and cool on a wire rack. Dust liberally with icing sugar and serve with poached pears and pouring cream.

180g butter
170g x 65% chocolate
170g caster sugar
6 eggs
200g ground almonds
15ml brandy
2 pinches salt
icing sugar
poached pears
250ml fresh cream

Poached Pears

POUR the red wine and water into a saucepan and add the brown sugar, cinnamon stick, star anise and cloves into a saucepan that fits the pears snuggly.

BRING the red wine to the boil, add the peeled pears, cover the pears with a disc of greaseproof paper. Bring the liquid to the boil and simmer for 20 minutes or until the pears are soft but still a little firm.

REMOVE the pan from the heat and set aside to cool, about 2 hours. Store the pears in the liquid until ready to use.

750ml red wine
450ml water
270g brown sugar
6 cinnamon stick
6 star anise
4 cloves
6 ripe pears

A Mediterranean
Breeze

{ Serves 8 }

Egg-fried Brinjal with Ginger, Chilli & Mint

Herbed Focaccia

Red Pepper, Roasted Onion & Thyme Salad

Lamb Pilaf with Red Peppers

Yoghurt Salad with Grapes, Walnuts & Cucumber

Chocolate-stuffed Prune & Almond Tart

Egg-fried Brinjal with Ginger, Chilli & Mint

WHISK the eggs, salt and pepper and stir in the thinly sliced brinjals. Heat a shallow layer of olive oil in a non-stick frying pan and fry the slices of brinjals dipped in the egg, in small batches until tender over medium heat.

LAY the cooked brinjals onto a platter. For the dressing, stir the olive oil, lemon oil, shredded ginger, juice of the lemon, chopped chilli, salt and pepper.

SPOON the dressing over the brinjals and scatter over the mint leaves.

2 eggs
salt and black pepper
2 brinjals
olive oil

Dressing

30ml olive oil
10ml lemon olive oil
5cm knob fresh ginger
juice of 1 lemon
1 red chilli
5 sprigs mint

Herbed Focaccia

WHISK the yeast with 150ml of lukewarm water until the yeast has dissolved. In another bowl pour in the olive oil, salt, sugar, 150ml of boiling water, and whisk until the sugar and salt have dissolved, then pour in the remaining water. Sieve the flour into a bowl, add the pesto, make a well in the centre and pour in most of the lukewarm liquid. Mix to a loose dough, adding the rest of the liquid if need be.

TIP the dough onto a lightly floured work surface and cover with a cloth and rest for 5 minutes. Then knead the dough for 10 minutes or until smooth, springy and elastic. Tip the dough into a lightly greased bowl, cover with clingfilm, and set aside to double in size. This will take about 45–60 minutes. Knock back the dough, tip onto a lightly floured work surface, cover with a cloth and rest for 10 minutes. Roll out the dough to 1cm thick, transfer to a lightly oiled baking tray and make indentations all over the surface with your fingers. Brush liberally with the garlic olive oil and sprinkle with sea salt. Loosely cover the dough with a dishcloth and set aside for 20–30 minutes.

PRE-HEAT the oven to 220°C. Place the focaccia in the oven for 5 minutes, turn down the oven to 200°C and bake for 15–20 minutes. Instead of the garlic olive oil, try using rosemary olive oil or chilli olive oil. As another alternative, omit the pesto and add pitted olives, pepperdews or grated Parmesan cheese.

THE dough can also be used for pizza bases. The bread is great for a nibble before dinner with marinated olives or roasted vegetables.

20g fresh yeast
425ml water
60ml olive oil
10ml sea salt
15g sugar
680g white bread flour
15ml pesto
garlic olive oil

Red Pepper, Roasted Onion & Thyme Salad

PRE-HEAT the oven to 200°C. Tip the chopped onions into a small roasting tray and season with salt, pepper, and drizzle with olive oil and roast until the onions have softened, about 35 minutes.

GRILL the peppers over an open flame until their skins are blackened, then put them in a bowl, cover with clingfilm and leave for 10 minutes or so. The skins will have wrinkled and be easy to peel. Roughly chop the peppers and the roasted onion, tip into a bowl and stir in the olive oil, vinegar, thyme leaves, paprika, salt and pepper.

SPREAD the salad on a plate, drizzle with extra olive oil and serve with the egg-fried brinjal and herbed focaccia. For a quick salad, use a tin of drained pimento peppers.

2 onions
salt and black pepper
2 red peppers
90ml olive oil
30ml sherry vinegar
2 sprigs thyme
10ml paprika (bittersweet)
rosemary olive oil

Lamb Pilaf with Red Peppers

SOAK the rice in water for 30 minutes. Heat the oil and butter in a saucepan and fry the chopped onion until softened, add the lamb cubes, season with salt, pepper and the cinnamon.

COVER the saucepan with a lid and cook for 10 minutes. Add the tomato purée, chopped parsley, chopped tomatoes, sliced red pepper, green olives, toasted pine nuts and raisins, then pour in enough water to cover the meat. Bring the liquid to the boil and cook on medium heat for 1½ hours or until the meat is tender.

THROW in the washed and drained rice, cover with 600ml of boiling water, bring to the boil, cover with a lid and simmer for 20 minutes. The rice should be tender.

SET aside for 10 minutes still covered, then serve.

450g basmati rice
45ml olive oil
45g butter
1 large onion
450g cubed lamb
salt and black pepper
5ml ground cinnamon
45ml tomato purèe
10g Italian parsley
2 large tomatoes
2 red peppers
100g green olives
30ml pine nuts
10g raisins

Yoghurt Salad with Grapes, Walnuts & Cucumber

STIR together the Greek yoghurt, grapes, seeded and chopped cucumber, toasted walnuts, mint leaves and parsley leaves.

SEASON with salt and pepper and transfer to a serving bowl. Serve with the lamb pilaf.

200g Greek yoghurt
250g seedless green grapes
1 English cucumber
100g walnuts
6 sprigs mint
10g Italian parsley
salt and black pepper

Chocolate-stuffed Prune & Almond Tart

TO make the pastry, tip the flour, chopped butter and caster sugar into a large mixing bowl. Rub the butter between your fingers until the mixture resembles fine breadcrumbs. Lightly whisk the egg yolks and milk and add to the flour mixture. Stir until the dough comes together. Tip the dough onto a lightly floured surface and bring the dough together to form a flattish ball. Wrap in clingfilm and place in the fridge for an hour.

PRE-HEAT the oven to 180°C. Roll out the pastry on a lightly floured surface to line a 30cm tart tin and prick the base of the tart with a fork. Place in the fridge for 10 minutes. Bake blind for 15 minutes or until cooked.

MEANWHILE make the topping: tip the prunes, 15ml of caster sugar and brandy in a saucepan and simmer for 5–10 minutes or until the prunes have absorbed the brandy, set aside to cool, then stuff each prune with broken chocolate.

CREAM the butter and sugar until pale, beat in the eggs one at a time until well incorporated, stir in the ground almonds. Spoon the almond filling into the cooked shell and scatter around the prunes, pressing down lightly. Bake the tart for 20–30 minutes or until coloured. Cool in the tin for 10 minutes before removing the tart.

Pastry

175g cake flour
90g butter
60g caster sugar
2 egg yolks
80ml milk

Filling

300g pitted dried prunes
175g caster sugar
175ml brandy
90g of 65% chocolate
175g butter
2 eggs
175g whole almonds, skins on

Jersey Cookout

Beef Hamburger with
Salted-Pickled Cucumbers

Spiced Brinjal Burger with Tomato Relish

Paprika-spiced Potato Wedges with Garlic Aioli

Bratwurst with Mustard

Creamy Sweet Potato & Spring Onion Salad

Sweet & Sour Coleslaw

Maple Pecan Pie with Vanilla Ice Cream

Beef Hamburger with Salted-Pickled Cucumbers

FOR the salt-pickled cucumbers, thinly slice the cucumbers and place them in a non-metallic bowl, stir together with the salt, rice vinegar and caster sugar, and set aside for 30 minutes. Drain the cucumbers and set aside. You can reserve the pickling solution in the fridge for another batch.

MIX the beef mince, crushed garlic, chopped onion, chopped rosemary, chopped oregano, egg, salt, pepper, seeded and chopped chilli and Worcestershire sauce together in a bowl, divide into 4 patties and set aside.

GRILL the burger patties for 10 minutes on each side, or to your liking, turning once only. Brush the halved Portuguese rolls with olive oil and grill on the braai until toasted.

ASSEMBLE each burger with lettuce, sliced tomato, beef patty and top with pickled cucumbers.

SERVE with paprika-spiced wedges, garlic aioli and sweet and sour coleslaw.

Salt-pickled Cucumbers

2 English cucumbers
10ml sea salt
100ml rice vinegar
60g caster sugar

Beef Patties

500g beef mince
2 garlic cloves
salt and black pepper
1 onion
1 sprig rosemary
2 sprigs oregano
1 egg
1 chilli
10ml Worcestershire sauce

To Serve

4 Portuguese rolls
half a butter lettuce
3 vine-ripened tomatoes

{ makes 4 burgers }

Spiced Brinjal Burger

PRE-HEAT the oven to 200°C. Chop the brinjals and place on a baking tray, season with salt and pepper, drizzle with chilli oil and crushed garlic, and roast for 25–30 minutes or until soft.

TIP the cooked brinjals into a mixing bowl, add the zest and juice of the lemon, and the drained chickpeas. Roughly mash together. Stir in the chopped spring onion, roughly ground cumin seeds, dried crushed chilli, chopped mint, chopped coriander, breadcrumbs, salt and pepper.

FORM the mixture into 4 burger patties, dust with flour and place in the fridge to firm up. Grill the burgers over coals or in a hot grill-pan for 5–10 minutes on each side. Brush the halved Portuguese rolls with olive oil and toast the cut side.

ASSEMBLE each burger with gem lettuce, spiced brinjal burger, sliced cherry tomatoes and homemade tomato relish (page 90). Serve with paprika-spiced wedges and garlic aioli and sweet and sour coleslaw.

2 brinjals
30ml chilli olive oil
1 garlic clove
zest and juice of half a lemon
400g tin chickpeas
half a bunch spring onions
5ml cumin seeds
2ml dried crushed chilli
2 sprigs mint leaves
10g coriander
75g fresh breadcrumbs
salt and black pepper
cake flour

To Serve

4 Portuguese rolls
1 gem lettuce
tomato relish
12 cherry tomatoes

{ makes 4 burgers }

Paprika-spiced Potato Wedges

PRE-HEAT the oven to 180°C. Cut the potatoes into wedges and toss together with the paprika, thyme leaves, olive oil, salt and pepper.

SCATTER onto a baking tray and roast for 40 minutes or until crispy and golden. Serve on a platter with garlic aioli separate.

8 baking potatoes
20ml sweet paprika
2 sprigs thyme
45ml olive oil
salt and black pepper

Garlic Aioli

PLACE the peeled garlic, egg yolks, Dijon mustard, salt and vinegar in a food processor and blitz until the garlic is smooth.

SLOWLY pour in the sunflower oil and olive oil until you have a thick, dropping consistency. Check the seasoning and store in the fridge until needed.

FOR different flavour variations, add paprika, pesto, chopped olives or wasabi.

4 garlic cloves
2 eggs yolks
2ml Dijon mustard
2ml salt
15ml white wine vinegar
125ml sunflower oil
100ml olive oil

Tomato Relish

COMBINE the chopped tomatoes, chopped red onion, crushed garlic, julienne ginger, ground allspice, mustard seeds, chilli powder, salt and white wine vinegar in a saucepan, bring to the boil and cook on medium heat for 20 minutes.

ADD the sugar and cook for another 40 minutes, stirring occasionally until thick.

POUR into sterilized jars, seal and store in pantry.
(Keeps for up to 3 months.)

750g tomatoes
half a red onion
2 garlic cloves
1 x 5cm knob ginger
2ml ground allspice
3ml mustard seeds
2ml chilli powder
5ml sea salt
100ml white wine vinegar
125g sugar

{ makes one litre }

Bratwurst with Mustard

GRILL the sausages on the braai, turning often, until evenly browned and cooked through. You could select weisswurst or any good German deli sausages. Cooking 2 wursts per person will ensure leftovers for snacks or lunch boxes.

SERVE with mustards, sweet and sour coleslaw, and creamy sweet potato, caper and spring onion salad.

2 bratwurst per person
German mustard
wholegrain mustard
sea salt

Creamy Sweet Potato, Caper & Spring Onion Salad

COOK the sweet potatoes in salted water for 45 minutes or until tender. Drain and leave to cool until you can handle them, then slice the potatoes into discs and tip into a mixing bowl.

FOR the dressing whisk the olive oil, vinegar, Dijon mustard, cream, salt and pepper together, stir in the capers, finely sliced red onion, chopped spring onion and dill tops.

WHILE the potatoes are still hot, pour the dressing over, carefully stir together and set aside for 30 minutes for the flavours to develop.

A great addition is to stir in sliced hard-boiled egg along with 2 chopped anchovies.

900g sweet potatoes
100ml olive oil
30ml red wine vinegar
30ml Dijon mustard
60ml cream
salt and black pepper
45ml capers
1 red onion
1 bunch spring onions
15ml dried dill tops

Sweet & Sour Coleslaw

IN a mixing bowl toss together the julienne cucumber, shredded cabbage and julienne carrots.

WHISK together the crushed garlic, crushed dried red chilli, balsamic vinegar, olive oil, sweet chilli sauce, salt and pepper. Check the seasoning and if you feel like extra heat, add a little more chilli.

TOSS everything together and stir in the chopped coriander.

2 English cucumbers
half a medium cabbage
4 carrots
1 garlic clove
2ml crushed dried red chilli
80ml balsamic vinegar
80ml olive oil
80ml sweet chilli sauce
salt and black pepper
10g coriander

Maple Pecan Pie with Vanilla Ice Cream

FOR the pastry, place the flour, chopped butter and caster sugar into a large mixing bowl. Rub the butter between your fingers until the mixture resembles fine breadcrumbs. Lightly whisk the egg yolk and milk together and add three-quarters to the flour mixture. You may not need all the liquid or you may need to add more. Stir until the dough comes together.

TIP the dough onto a lightly floured surface and bring the dough together to form a flattish ball. Wrap in clingfilm and place in the fridge for an hour. Pre-heat the oven to 180°C. Roll out the pastry on a lightly floured surface to line a 24cm tart tin and prick the base of the tart with a fork. Place in the fridge for 10 minutes.

BAKE blind for 15 minutes or until cooked. Meanwhile, make the filling by whisking the sugar, softened butter, eggs, maple syrup, golden syrup and vanilla extract together. Last, stir in the pecan nuts, then scrape the filling into the cooked shell. Bake the tart for 20–30 minutes or until set. Cool in the tin for 10 minutes before removing the tart and serve with vanilla ice cream.

Pastry

180g cake flour
90g butter
60g caster sugar
2 egg yolks
80ml milk

Filling

115g caster sugar
30g butter
3 eggs
125ml maple syrup
85ml golden syrup
5ml vanilla extract
175g pecan nuts

Vanilla Ice Cream

HEAT the cream, milk and vanilla bean paste until just starting to boil. Whisk the egg yolks and sugar together until pale, pour in half the hot cream, whisk until smooth, then pour the eggy cream back into the saucepan. Cook on medium heat, stirring until the mixture thickens and coats the back of a spoon.

STRAIN the custard, allow it to cool and then chill it in the fridge. Churn the custard in an ice-cream machine until thick: it should be difficult to stir. Scrape out into an airtight container and freeze for at least an hour before using.

IF you don't have an ice-cream machine, simply freeze the mixture in an airtight container, and stir vigorously with a fork every 20 minutes or until set.

300ml cream
300ml milk
3ml vanilla bean paste
6 egg yolks
150g caster sugar

{ makes 750ml }

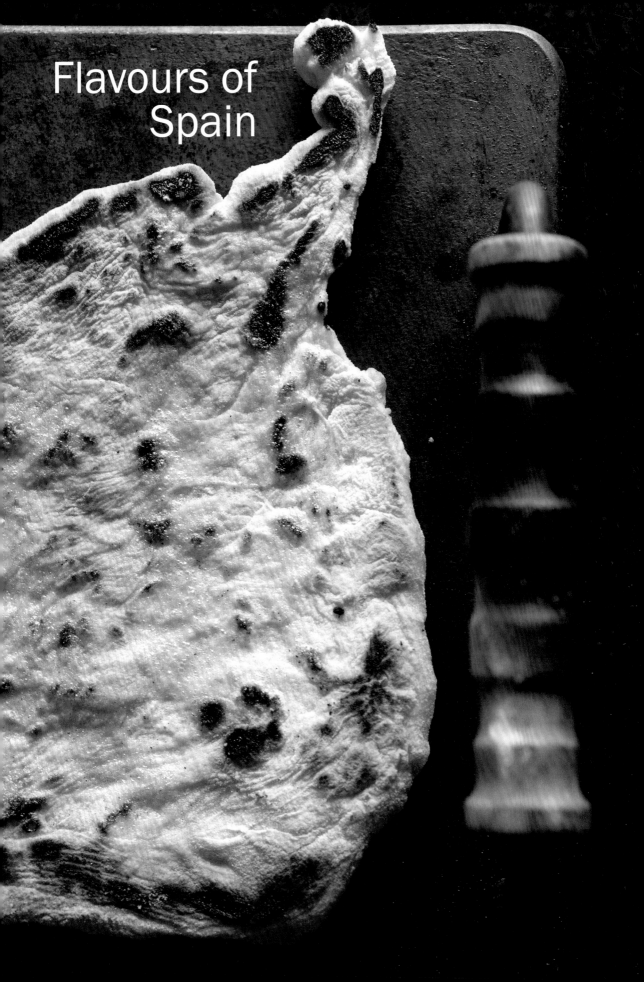

Flavours of
Spain

{ Serves 8 }

Moroccan Flat Breads

Tomato Stuffed with Tuna, Garlic & Parsley

Chicken Meatballs with Saffron Almond Sauce

BBQ Quail with Sweet & Sour Syrup

Avocado Salad with Almond Taratar

Sweet Buñuelos with Orange Curd

Moroccan Flat Breads

MIX the bread flour, salt, water, yeast and olive oil together in the bowl of your cake mixer, and knead at medium speed using the paddle attachment, for 5 minutes.

COVER the bowl with clingfilm and leave to rest for one hour. Divide the dough into 8 equal pieces. Roll one piece out at a time to a 16cm round.

HEAT a large cast-iron frying pan over medium heat, place a knob of butter and melt. Place one sheet of dough into pan, and fry until brown patches begin to form underneath, turn heat down if it begins to burn. Put another knob of butter in pan, turn bread over, and cook the other side.

PLACE in a warm dish in the oven until all the breads are cooked.

250g stoneground flour
2.5ml salt
185g warm water
5g dried instant yeast
15ml olive oil

{ makes 8 breads }

Tomato Stuffed with Tuna, Garlic & Parsley

TO make the tomato sauce, tip the tomato juice, peeled and finely chopped onion, finely chopped celery, crushed garlic, tomato purée, olive oil, sugar, salt and pepper into a saucepan and bring to the boil. Simmer for 20 minutes or until thick and jammy, check the seasoning and purée.

TO make the aioli, mix the peeled and crushed garlic and egg in a small blender and then slowly pour in the sunflower oil, a little at a time, until the mixture is thick and creamy. Add lemon juice, salt and pepper to taste.

ABOUT an hour before serving, prepare the tuna stuffing by combining the tuna, 40ml of the tomato sauce, 30ml aioli, 20ml pesto, salt and pepper. Stir until combined and set aside.

BLANCH, peel and seed the tomatoes. Fill each one with the tuna stuffing and place upside down on a serving plate. To make the vinaigrette, whisk the oil and vinegar together, season with salt and pepper, drizzle the tomatoes with the remaining pesto and then with the vinaigrette.

Tomato Sauce

400g tomato juice
half an onion
1 stick celery
3 garlic cloves
15ml tomato purée
45ml olive oil
7ml caster sugar

Aioli

1 garlic clove
1 egg
100ml sunflower oil
lemon juice to taste
salt and black pepper
a little milk

150g tin tuna in olive oil
75ml pesto
8 small ripe tomatoes
20ml balsamic vinegar

Chicken Meatballs in a Saffron Almond Sauce

FOR the meatballs, tip the chicken mince into a bowl and stir in the breadcrumbs, crushed garlic, egg, chopped parsley, lemon zest, salt and pepper together and roll into about 12 meatballs and set aside. To make saffron almond sauce, heat 30ml of olive oil in a saucepan over medium heat, then add the almonds and cook, stirring, for 5 minutes, or until golden.

REMOVE with a slotted spoon, tip into a mortar and pestle. To the saucepan add the chopped onion to the pan and cook for 5 minutes, or until soft, add the bay leaf, crushed garlic, cumin, cinnamon, paprika and clove and cook for one minute, or until fragrant. Add the wine, Marsala wine, stock and saffron, bring to the boil and allow to boil for 2 minutes, or until reduced to a thick sauce. Take the pan off the heat, discard the clove and bay leaf, and set aside while cooking the meatballs.

TIP the egg yolk into the almonds and pound to paste and stir into the hot sauce, then spoon into a bowl. Heat a little oil in a frying pan, and cook the meatballs for 12 minutes, or until just cooked through and browned all over. Serve with the saffron sauce on the side for dipping.

THE egg white can be chopped up and used for garnishing the saffron sauce.

Chicken Meatballs

250g chicken mince
60g fresh sourdough breadcrumbs
1 garlic clove
1 egg
10g Italian parsley
zest of half a lemon

Saffron Almond Sauce

olive oil
20 almonds
half a small red onion
1 fresh bay leaf
2 garlic cloves
2.5ml ground cumin
2ml ground cinnamon
2ml hot smoked paprika
1 clove
30ml white wine
30ml Marsala wine
125ml chicken stock
2ml saffron
1 hard-boiled egg

BBQ Quail with Sweet & Sour Syrup

COMBINE sliced onion, saffron, cinnamon, ginger, crushed cardamom, olive oil and quail together, cover with clingfilm and set aside for 30 minutes to marinate or overnight in the fridge.

FOR syrup, pour the verjuice, molasses and lemon juice in a small saucepan. Bring the sauce to the boil and simmer for 5 minutes or until syrupy, then set aside.

HEAT a grill pan over medium-high heat. Thread a quail onto skewers and cook for 5 minutes on each side or until golden and cooked through.

REMOVE the skewer and cut each quail in half and serve the quails drizzled with syrup and a wedge of lemon. The quails are great cooked on the braai.

1 small onion
pinch of saffron
2.5ml ground cinnamon
2.5ml ground ginger
2.5ml ground cardamom
30ml olive oil
4 de-boned quails
1 lemon

Sweet & Sour Syrup

80ml verjuice
30ml pomegranate molasses
15ml lemon juice

Avocado Salad with Almond Taratar

FOR the taratar, blitz the almonds in a food processor until roughly chopped. Add the crushed garlic, salt, pepper, lemon juice, vinegar, honey and egg yolks and blitz until creamy and smooth. With the motor running, slowly drizzle in half the olive oil, followed by half the water to loosen and stabilize the mixture. Slowly drizzle in the rest of the olive oil to form a thick, creamy mayonnaise. Add more water if it is too thick.

JUST before serving, cut each avocado in half and carefully remove the stone. Using a large spoon, scoop the avocado halves out of their skins. Arrange the salad leaves on a platter with the avocado. Whisk the taratar and spoon into each avocado cavity. Sprinkle with freshly cracked black pepper and serve.

Taratar

75g blanched almonds
1 garlic clove
salt and black pepper
juice of half a lemon
20ml sherry vinegar
5ml honey
1 egg yolk
125ml olive oil
20ml lukewarm water

Salad

4 ripe avocados
100g mixed salad leaves

Sweet Buñuelos with Orange Curd

PRE-HEAT the oven to 180°C. Combine the water with the oil, orange zest, sugar and salt in a small saucepan and stir until the sugar has dissolved. Bring just to the boil over a high heat. Remove and tip in the sifted flour, stirring to form a smooth paste that comes away from the side of the pan. If the oil separates, the mixture is overheated and you need to start again.

REMOVE from the heat, cool slightly, then gradually stir in the beaten eggs with a wooden spoon until very well combined. Continue beating for a few minutes until the mixture is thick, glossy and smooth. Line 2 baking trays with baking paper. Divide the dough into 8 even-sized mounds, 4 to a tray.

BAKE for 10 minutes, or until puffed, then reduce the oven temperature to 180°C and cook for 15 minutes, or until crisp and golden. Remove from the oven and pierce a small hole in each base to let the steam escape. Cool on a cake rack.

MAKE the cream filling by whisking the cream, vanilla extract and icing sugar in a bowl until soft peaks form. Split the puffs in half. Dollop a spoon of orange curd over the bases, then the cream filling. Replace the tops, then sift the cinnamon sugar over and serve at once.

Sweet Buñuelos

90ml water
60ml extra virgin olive oil
zest of half an orange
5ml caster sugar
pinch of salt
60g cake flour
2 eggs

Filling

170ml cream
5ml vanilla extract
15ml icing sugar

1 jar orange curd
cinnamon sugar

Greek Accents

Smoked Mackerel Dip

Slow-cooked Lamb with
Potatoes & White Wine

Simple Greek Salad

Tzatziki

Zucchini Fritters

Chestnut & Cinnamon Cake
with Roasted Plums

{ Serves 8 }

Smoked Mackerel Dip

FLAKE the smoked mackerel into a bowl and remove the bones. Stir in the olive oil, lemon juice, chopped dill, yoghurt, cream cheese, salt and black pepper.

CHECK the seasoning and scrape the dip onto a platter, drizzle with extra olive oil and crushed chilli. Serve with sliced crusty bread. The dip works just as well with smoked snoek, and you can add chopped parsley with the dill for extra depth of flavour.

350g smoked mackerel
60ml olive oil
juice of 1 lemon
10g dill
75g Greek yoghurt
100g smooth cream cheese
salt and black pepper
2ml crushed dried chilli

Slow-cooked Lamb with Potatoes & White Wine

PRE-HEAT the oven to 160°C. Brown the leg of lamb in olive oil over a high heat, turning often, until golden in colour.

TIP in the sliced garlic, wedges of lemon, white wine, water, halved potatoes, rosemary, thyme and bay leaves, season with salt and pepper.

COVER the pot with a lid and roast for 3 hours. Roughly shred the lamb and serve on a platter with the potatoes and juices. Serve with simple Greek salad, tzatziki and zucchini fritters.

1.5kg leg of lamb
1 head of garlic
1 lemon
300ml white wine
400ml water
8 Mediterranean potatoes
2 sprigs rosemary
4 sprigs thyme
4 bay leaves
salt and black pepper

Simple Greek Salad

ON a plate, scatter the chopped tomatoes, skinned and chopped cucumber, sliced onion, olives, and season with salt and pepper.

LAY the sliced feta in the centre, drizzle over the olive oil, sprinkle over the dried oregano and serve with wedges of lemon.

3 tomatoes
2 English cucumbers
half a red onion
100g kalamata olives
100g feta cheese
45ml olive oil
salt and black pepper
2ml dried oregano
2 lemons

Tzatziki

STRAIN the yoghurt in a muslin-lined colander the day before you want to make the tzatziki.

GRATE the cucumber and squeeze out the excess water. Stir the yoghurt together with the olive oil, vinegar, crushed garlic and dried cucumber.

CHECK the seasoning and serve sprinkled with chopped fennel.

400g Greek yoghurt
2 English cucumbers
35ml olive oil
2ml white wine vinegar
5 garlic cloves
1 sprig fennel
salt and black pepper

Zucchini Fritters

GRATE the baby marrow, tip into a bowl and stir together with the chopped spring onion, chopped parsley, chopped mint, finely chopped haloumi cheese, beaten eggs, salt, pepper and cake flour.

HEAT the olive oil in a frying pan and fry spoonfuls of the fritters until golden in colour.

500g baby marrow
3 spring onions
5g Italian parsley
4 sprigs mint
70g haloumi cheese
2 eggs
salt and black pepper
80ml cake flour
80ml olive oil

Chestnut & Cinnamon Cake with Roasted Plums

PRE-HEAT the oven to 180°C. Place the plums in a casserole dish, and sprinkle with sugar and pour over the water and wine. Roast for 20 minutes, basting after 10 minutes. Remove and cool.

LINE the base of a 20cm spring-form cake tin with greaseproof paper. Grease with a little butter and dust with cake flour.

TIP the chestnut purée into a small pan with the water and warm gently. Once melted, beat in the softened butter and cinnamon. Whisk the egg whites until stiff and set aside. Whisk the yolks and sugars until pale in colour. Fold the chestnut purée into the egg yolk, and then fold in the egg whites.

SCRAPE into the prepared cake tin and bake at 180°C for 40 minutes until an inserted skewer comes away clean. Cool in the tin for 10 minutes and then unmould and cool on a wire rack. Dust with icing sugar and serve with poached plums.

Plums

6 plums
50g brown sugar
50ml water
50ml dessert wine

Cake

435g tin of chestnut purée
60ml water
25g butter
5ml ground cinnamon
3 eggs
100g caster sugar
50g brown sugar
icing sugar to finish

Alfresco Lunch

{ Serves 8 }

Herb-roasted Chicken Breast Salad

Pickled Cucumber with Steamed Trout

Roasted Beetroot Salad with Lentil Dressing

Cherry Tomato, Potato & Olive Salad

Carrot, Mustard Seed & Feta Salad

Blueberry Cream Cake

Herb-roasted Chicken Breast Salad

PRE-HEAT the oven to 180°C. Finely grind the coriander and fennel seeds in a mortar and pestle, then add the chopped parsley, rosemary leaves, sage leaves, sunflower oil and the 5ml freshly ground black pepper, until you have a pesto-like paste. Marinate the chicken breasts in the herb oil for at least 2 hours or overnight.

WHEN ready to cook, wrap each breast in the pancetta. Heat a frying pan that can go in the oven and seal the chicken breasts on both sides, pour in the verjuice and roast for 20–25 minutes or until tender.

COOL the chicken for 10 minutes and serve with wedges of lemon.

15ml coriander seeds
15ml fennel seeds
2 sprigs Italian parsley
2 sprigs rosemary
2 sprigs sage
5ml sunflower oil
8 chicken breast fillets
8 slices pancetta
250ml verjuice
olive oil
2 lemons

Pickled Cucumber with Steamed Trout

PORTION the trout into 8 pieces and steam in a bamboo steamer over a pan of boiling water for 5–8 minutes until just cooked, then set aside.

FOR the cucumber salad, whisk the vinegar and sugar together until the sugar has dissolved. Shave ribbons of cucumber with a potato peeler, then stir in the vinegar, chopped dill, salt and pepper, and set aside for 10 minutes.

DRAIN the cucumber, lay on a platter, top with the poached trout, and garnish with a few grindings of black pepper.

1kg smoked rainbow trout
salt and black pepper

Cucumber Salad

100ml white wine vinegar
100ml caster sugar
4 sprigs dill
2 English cucumbers

Roasted Beetroot Salad with Lentil Dressing

PRE-HEAT the oven to 180°C. Place the halved beetroot in a baking tray and season with salt, pepper and olive oil. Cover with tin foil and roast for 45–90 minutes or until the beetroots are tender. Time varies according to the age and season of the beetroot.

FOR the dressing, whisk the vinegar, olive oil, oregano olive oil, sugar, 45ml water, salt and pepper together and add the drained lentils. Pour the dressing over beetroot and garnish with snipped chives.

1kg beetroot
salt and black pepper
50ml olive oil
30ml red wine vinegar
30ml olive oil
15ml oregano olive oil
2.5ml caster sugar
410g tin lentils
10g chives

Cherry Tomato, Potato & Olive Salad

COOK the potatoes in salted water until tender, drain, refresh in water and cool until you can peel them.

WHILE the potatoes are still warm, add the halved cherry tomatoes, chopped mint leaves, olive oil, roughly chopped anchovies, olives, verjuice, salt and pepper.

STIR the ingredients together well and set aside for at least 30 minutes before serving to allow the flavours to develop.

20 new potatoes
250g cherry tomatoes
1 bunch mint
60ml olive oil
8 anchovies
100ml kalamata olives
60ml verjuice
salt and black pepper

Carrot, Mustard Seed & Feta Salad

HEAT the olive oil in a frying pan. Trim the carrots and cut into quarters lengthways and fry in the hot oil. Cook the carrots, stirring occasionally for 8–10 minutes; once they start to colour add the mustard seeds, cook for a couple of minutes, then pour in 100ml boiling water, brown sugar, salt and pepper.

COOK the carrots until no liquid remains, stir in the vinegar, tip onto a serving plate, crumble over the feta and drizzle over a little olive oil.

30ml olive oil
450g carrots
30ml yellow mustard seeds
30ml brown sugar
salt and black pepper
30ml black vinegar
200g Danish feta

Blueberry Cream Cake

FIRST make the custard: in a food processor blitz the milk, vanilla bean paste, egg yolks, sugar and flour until smooth, then scrape into a saucepan. Whisk over medium heat; as soon as it comes to the boil, remove from the heat and cool.

PRE-HEAT the oven to 180°C. Line the base of a 20cm spring-form cake tin with greaseproof paper. Lightly grease with butter and dust with flour.

FOR the shortcake: stir the blueberries with the wine; once the custard is cool, gently fold in the marinating blueberries. Blitz the flour, salt and butter for a minute in a food processor until the mixture resembles fine breadcrumbs, add the egg yolks, eggs, sugar, and the zest and juice of a lemon. Blitz again until the dough comes together, press two-thirds of the dough into the tin top with the blueberry custard, leaving 2cm edge around the edge.

PAT out the rest of the dough to make a lid and place over the filling, brush with a little milk, sprinkle over extra caster sugar and bake for 50–60 minutes or until an inserted skewer comes away clean.

COOL in the tin for 10 minutes. Place the cake onto a plate and dust with icing sugar and serve.

Custard
225ml milk
2ml vanilla bean paste
2 egg yolks
30ml caster sugar
15ml cake flour

Shortcake
250g blueberries
30ml white wine
350g cake flour
2ml salt
200g butter
1 egg
2 egg yolks
200g caster sugar
1 lemon

A Moroccan Twist

{ Serves 6 }

Split Pea Cakes with Cherry Tomato
& Sunflower Seed Salad

Sweet Potato, Pea, Asparagus & Almond Salad

Sweet & Sour Chickpeas

Moroccan Chicken
with Moroccan Tomato Sauce

Exotic Fruit Salad with Raspberry
& Lemongrass Sorbet

Split Pea Cakes with Cherry Tomato & Sunflower Seed Salad

SOAK the split peas overnight in water. Drain and wash the peas and tip the drained peas into a food processor with the chopped garlic, ginger, lemon zest, turmeric, cumin, chilli powder, salt, chopped spring onion, milk, bicarbonate of soda and flour, and blitz until smooth. Scrape into a bowl and set aside.

HEAT a frying pan with oil to shallow-fry the split pea cakes, drop spoonfuls of the mix into the hot oil and cook for a couple of minutes before turning over. The mix will make about 36 cakes.

ROUGHLY chop the tomatoes and tip into a bowl, season with salt, pepper, balsamic reduction and olive oil, and set aside. When you are ready to serve, toss the coriander leaves and watercress with the tomatoes, arrange on a platter, top with the split pea cakes, dollop with the yoghurt and sprinkle over the sunflower seeds.

SPLIT pea cakes are great in a pita pocket or in a wrap.

Cakes

250ml split peas
2 garlic cloves
5cm knob fresh ginger
zest of half a lemon
5ml turmeric
10ml ground cumin
2ml chilli powder
5ml salt
half a bunch spring onions
200ml milk
3ml bicarbonate of soda
100g self-raising flour
sunflower oil

Salad

250g cherry tomatoes
salt & black pepper
15ml balsamic reduction
30ml olive oil
20g coriander leaves
1 bunch watercress
100ml Greek yoghurt
60ml toasted sunflower seeds

Sweet Potato, Pea, Asparagus & Almond Salad

CUT the sweet potatoes into discs and boil in salted water until tender, drain and set aside.

TO make the dressing, lightly whisk the orange zest and juice, fromage frais, yoghurt, walnut oil, salt and pepper together.

COMBINE the drained sweet potato, blanched asparagus, cooked peas, rocket, toasted almonds, coriander leaves, snipped chives, toasted and ground Szechwan in a large bowl. When you are ready to serve, toss together well with the dressing. Arrange on a platter and serve.

4 sweet potatoes

Dressing

zest and juice of 2 oranges
60ml fromage frais
30ml natural yoghurt
45ml walnut oil
salt and black pepper

Salad

250g frozen peas
1 bunch asparagus
250g rocket
12 whole almonds
10g coriander
10g chives
5ml Szechwan peppercorns

Sweet & Sour Chickpeas

COVER the chickpeas with water and soak overnight. The following day, drain the chickpeas and tip into a medium saucepan. Cover with water. Bring to the boil and simmer until tender. This will take about 40 minutes. Remove any scum that floats to the surface. Drain the chickpeas and tip into a bowl.

HEAT the oil in a saucepan and fry the sliced onion until soft, then stir in the chopped ginger. Add the chickpeas, sugar, coriander, cumin, chilli powder, garam masala, salt and pepper. Stir, then add the tamarind, chopped tomato and water and simmer for 2–3 minutes. Bring to the boil and cook until the sauce has thickened. Stir in the chopped coriander leaves and serve.

400g chickpeas
30ml sunflower oil
2 onions
5cm knob fresh ginger
10ml sugar
10ml ground coriander
10ml ground cumin
pinch of chilli powder (optional)
5ml garam masala
salt and black pepper
45ml tamarind concentrate
400g tin chopped tomatoes
500ml water
10g coriander

Moroccan Chicken Served with Moroccan Tomato Sauce

TIP the peeled garlic, toasted cumin seeds, chopped chilli, paprika and yoghurt into a blender and blitz until smooth. Pour over the chicken breasts and marinate for a minimum of 30 minutes or up to 6 hours.

FOR the Moroccan tomato sauce, fry the chopped onion in olive oil in a saucepan for a couple of minutes, add the crushed garlic, chopped ginger, pepper, cayenne pepper, crushed cardamom seeds, cinnamon, coriander, cumin, tinned tomatoes, brown sugar, salt and pepper. Bring to the boil and simmer for 10–12 minutes or until reduced and thick.

HEAT a grill pan and scrape off any excess marinade off the chicken and grill for 10–15 minutes or until the chicken is cooked through. Serve with the warm Moroccan sauce, and garnish with toasted almonds and fresh coriander leaves

Moroccan Chicken

4 garlic cloves
15ml cumin seeds
1 chilli
10ml paprika
150ml natural yoghurt
6 skinned chicken breast fillets

Moroccan Tomato Sauce

15ml olive oil
1 small onion
1 garlic clove
5cm knob ginger
2ml ground black pepper
1ml cayenne pepper
5ml cardamom seeds
10ml ground cinnamon
5ml ground coriander
5ml ground cumin
400g tin chopped tomatoes
15ml brown sugar
50g flaked almonds
10g fresh coriander

Exotic Fruit Salad with a Raspberry & Lemongrass Sorbet

FOR the sorbet, place the caster sugar, water and chopped lemongrass in a saucepan to make a sugar syrup. Boil for 10 minutes, remove from the heat and allow to cool.

PLACE the raspberries in a blender along with the lemon juice and sugar syrup, and blitz until smooth. Strain the syrup into a bowl and place in the fridge to chill.

POUR the raspberry syrup in an ice-cream maker and churn until just set or scrape into a container and freeze for 30 minutes before use.

FOR the fruit salad, cut the fruit roughly the same size, spoon the fruit salad onto 6 plates and top with a spoon of the raspberry sorbet. For the sorbet we use frozen raspberries that have been thawed, although you could try using different berries, such as cranberries or mixed berries. For the exotic fruit salad any fruit can be used, such as banana, apple, pears and grapes.

Sorbet

450g caster sugar
600ml water
8 lemongrass stalks
450g raspberries
juice of 1 lemon

Fruit

guavas
kiwi fruit
strawberries
gooseberries
red currants
blueberries
pineapple
paw paw/papino
grapes

Lunch in Lebanon

{ Serves 8 }

Avocado & Tahini Dip

Stuffed Calamari with Dukkah

Orange & Cucumber Salad
with Orange Blossom Water

Lamb Fetteh

Roasted Pumpkin, Dried Oregano
& Bean Salad

Vanilla Yoghurt Panacotta
with Honey-poached Strawberries

Avocado & Tahini Dip

SCOOP the flesh out of the avocados and tip into a food processor with the lemon juice, tahini, olive oil, crushed garlic, salt, pepper and mint leaves, and blitz until smooth.

SCRAPE into bowls, garnish with the zatar spice and drizzle with a little olive oil.

GRILL the tortillas over an open flame and serve warm with the avocado and tahini dip.

2 ripe avocados
juice of 1 lemon
15ml tahini
45ml olive oil
1 garlic clove
salt and black pepper
30ml chopped mint
10ml zatar spice
2 tortilla wraps

Stuffed Calamari with Dukkah

RINSE the calamari in water, remove any cartilage and set aside.

HEAT half the olive oil in a frying pan and fry the finely chopped onion, crushed garlic and bay leaves, cook until just starting to caramelise. Add the dukkah, pour in half the Marsala wine and reduce until the wine has evaporated.

REMOVE from the heat and stir in the chopped parsley, peeled and chopped egg, salt and pepper. Once the stuffing is cold, stuff the calamari about two-thirds full and secure the end with a toothpick.

HEAT a frying pan that is big enough to hold the calamari in a single layer. Heat the remaining olive oil and brown the calamari on all sides, pour in the remaining Marsala wine, water, salt and pepper, simmer for 5 minutes or until the liquid has evaporated and thickened.

200g calamari tubes
80ml olive oil
1 onion
2 garlic cloves
2 bay leaves
30ml dukkah spice
200ml Marsala wine
10g Italian parsley
2 hard-boiled eggs
50ml water
salt and black pepper

Orange & Cucumber Salad with Orange Blossom Water

LAY the peeled and sliced oranges on a platter, top with the chopped cucumber, scatter over the finely sliced red onion.

WHISK the orange blossom water, olive oil and brown sugar together and drizzle over the salad.

SEASON with salt and pepper and scatter the fresh mint on top of the salad.

3 oranges
1 Lebanese cucumber
half a red onion
salt and black pepper
15ml orange blossom water
30ml extra virgin olive oil
5ml brown sugar
6 sprigs mint

Lamb Fetteh

COVER the chickpeas with water and soak overnight. The following day, drain and tip into a medium saucepan. Cover with water. Bring to the boil and simmer until tender; this will take about 40 minutes. Remove any scum that floats to the surface. Drain the chickpeas and set aside.

PRE-HEAT the oven to 180°C. Heat olive oil in a large casserole, brown the lamb. Add a cinnamon stick, allspice, white pepper, parsley stalks, a sliced onion and garlic halved width-ways, cover with 1½ litres water and bring to the boil, then simmer. Cover and cook for 2½ hours or until the meat falls from the bone. Remove meat from bone and set aside. Strain stock and reserve, discarding solids.

FOR yoghurt sauce, mix the yoghurt, crushed garlic, lemon juice, salt and pepper, check the seasoning and set aside. Pre-heat the oven to 180°C.

CUT the tortillas into quarters, scatter onto a baking tray, drizzle with olive oil, season with salt and pepper, and bake for 5 minutes or until golden in colour. Mix the lamb and chickpeas in an ovenproof baking dish, add 125ml reserved stock and cook for 10 minutes or until hot.

TO serve, top lamb with the toasted bread, drizzle with yoghurt sauce, scatter with roughly chopped parsley, sumac, toasted almonds and olives.

150g dried chickpeas
30ml olive oil
750g leg of lamb
1 cinnamon stick
5ml whole allspice
5ml white peppercorns
20 parsley stalks
3 onions
1 head of garlic
2 pita breads
60ml chopped parsley
5ml ground sumac
60ml flaked almonds
15ml olive oil
20 kalamata olives

Yoghurt Sauce

200ml natural yoghurt
1 clove of garlic
juice of half a lemon

Roasted Pumpkin, Dried Oregano & Bean Salad

COVER the beans with water and soak overnight. The following day, drain and tip into a medium saucepan. Cover with water. Bring to the boil and simmer until tender; this will take about 40 minutes. Remove any scum that floats to the surface. Drain the beans and set aside.

PRE-HEAT the oven to 180°C. Roast the cubed pumpkin with salt, pepper, olive oil and dried oregano for 30–45 minutes or until tender.

FOR the dressing, lightly whisk together the chopped flesh of the preserved lemon, olive oil, vinegar, honey, paprika, chopped parsley, salt and pepper. Toss with the drained beans and pumpkin.

100g dried butter beans
1.2kg pumpkin
2ml dried oregano
30ml olive oil
salt and black pepper

Dressing

1 preserved lemon
80ml olive oil
20ml sherry vinegar
20ml honey
10ml bittersweet paprika
10g Italian parsley

Vanilla Yoghurt Panacotta with Honey-poached Strawberries

SOAK the gelatine leaves in cold water for 5 minutes. Heat the cream gently. Tip the honey, orange juice, Greek yoghurt and vanilla into a mixing bowl and whisk together. Remove the warm cream from the heat, squeeze all the water out of the softened gelatine and add the gelatine to the warm cream. Lightly whisk together to dissolve the gelatine, then whisk into the yoghurt mixture.

POUR the liquid into a jug and divide into 6 dariole moulds. Set in the fridge for a minimum of 3 hours. For the poached strawberries, tip honey, verjuice and lemon peel into a small saucepan and bring to the boil. Hull the strawberries and cut them in half lengthways. Remove the verjuice liquid from the heat and add the hulled strawberries. Cool the strawberries and liquid, and place in the fridge until needed.

UNMOULD each panacotta onto a plate. To unmould, run a knife round the edge of the dish and invert the dish onto your hand giving a firm shake. Another way is to place the dish in hot water for a couple of seconds, then try tipping it out onto a plate with a firm shake.

SPOON the poached strawberries around the panacotta and serve. Use teacups if you don't have dariole moulds.

2½ gelatine leaves
150ml cream
75ml fynbos honey
45ml orange juice
425ml Greek yoghurt
15ml vanilla bean paste

Poached Strawberries

100ml honey
100ml verjuice
1 strip lemon peel
1 punnet strawberries

Thai Island Style

Chicken Satay
with Peanut Sauce

Chilli Sauce

Beef Penang

Coconut Rice

Cucumber Salad with Toasted Rice

Stir-fried Green Beans
& Sesame Seeds

Mint Ice Cream with Ginger Biscuits

Chicken Satay with Peanut Sauce

CUT each chicken breast into four strips lengthways and set aside. In a mortar and pestle pound the chopped onion, sliced garlic, coriander roots and sliced ginger to a paste.

ADD your paste to the chicken and stir in the ground coriander, cumin, turmeric, curry powder, light soy sauce, sunflower oil, coconut milk, sugar and salt. Mix together well, cover with clingfilm and place in the fridge overnight.

SOAK the bamboo sticks in water for an hour to prevent them from burning during cooking. The next day, thread a piece of chicken onto each skewer. Heat the grill of the oven, line a baking tray with tin foil and lay the chicken skewers side by side.

SEASON with salt and cook under the grill for 5 minutes, turn over and cook for another 5 minutes or until the chicken is cooked through and slightly charred. Serve hot with peanut sauce.

6 skinned chicken breast fillets
24 bamboo sticks
peanut sauce

Marinade

half an onion
3 garlic cloves
2 coriander roots
2.5cm knob of ginger
5ml ground coriander
5ml ground cumin
5ml ground turmeric
10ml Thai curry powder
30ml light soy sauce
60ml vegetable oil
150ml coconut milk
15ml palm sugar
5ml sea salt

{ makes 24 satays }

Peanut Sauce

HEAT sunflower oil in a saucepan and fry the crushed garlic, chopped onion and chopped white of the lemon-grass for a minute. Add the Thai curry powder, tamarind concentrate, chilli paste, chopped peanuts, coconut milk and sugar, and bring slowly to the boil. Add enough boiling water until you have a spoonable sauce consistency and simmer for 2 minutes. Season with salt and blitz in a food processor for 2 minutes.

LEFT-OVER peanut sauce is great on roasted sweet potatoes with coriander, or stir into shredded cabbage, mint and coriander leaves with garlic aioli for an Asian coleslaw.

15ml sunflower oil
2 garlic cloves
half an onion
1 stalk of lemon grass
10ml Thai curry powder
10ml tamarind concentrate
10ml chilli paste
60g unsalted roasted peanuts
180ml coconut milk
5ml palm sugar

{ Makes 180g }

Chilli Jam

HEAT the oil in a saucepan and fry the chopped onion and crushed garlic until soft. Add the chilli, brown sugar and a little salt. Bring to the boil, simmer for 2 minutes, remove from the heat and cool.

POUR into a sterilised bottle and keep in the fridge until needed. This is great stirred into mayonnaise or cream cheese.

80ml sunflower oil
half an onion
2 garlic cloves
40g dried crushed chilli
60ml brown sugar

{ Makes 185ml }

Beef Penang

TIP the peanuts into a saucepan, cover with water and simmer for 30 minutes or until soft, then drain and set aside.

BLITZ the chopped chilli, salt, chopped ginger, chopped onion, chopped lemongrass, peeled garlic and crushed nutmeg in a food processor to a paste. Add the drained peanuts and blitz to a purée.

TIP the coconut cream into a hot saucepan and heat. Once the cream starts to split, add 100ml of the paste and fry the paste for 10 minutes. Add the palm sugar and stir to dissolve. Pour in the fish sauce, coconut milk, chicken stock, lime leaves and seeded chillies and bring to the boil. Add the sliced beef and simmer for 10–15 minutes. Stir in the peas and basil, and serve.

FOR a lighter, healthier alternative, use beef or chicken stock instead of the coconut milk. Serve the beef penang with coconut rice, cucumber relish with toasted rice and chilli jam.

Paste

60ml raw peanuts
7 long dried red chillies
2ml salt
5cm knob ginger
1 red onion
2 stalks of lemongrass
4 garlic cloves
half a nutmeg

Beef

1 tin coconut cream
60ml palm sugar
2 tins coconut milk
500ml chicken stock
60ml fish sauce
9 Thai lime leaves
3 long red chillies
900g beef fillet
500ml frozen peas
10g basil leaves

Thai Curry Powder

DRY-ROAST the peppercorns, cloves, coriander, cumin and fennel seeds one ingredient at a time, in a frying pan over a low heat. Once fragrant, remove the spice and roast the next ingredient.

TRANSFER to a coffee grinder or pestle and mortar and grind to a powder. Stir in the remaining ingredients. Store in an airtight container.

10ml black peppercorns
10ml white peppercorns
10ml cloves
45ml coriander seeds
45ml cumin seeds
15ml fennel seeds
seeds from 8 cardamom pods
45m crushed chilli
30ml ground ginger
45ml ground turmeric

{ Makes 125g }

Coconut Rice

WASH the rice in running water until clean, cover with water and soak for one hour before draining thoroughly.

HEAT the oil in a saucepan and fry the rice for 3 minutes. Pour in the coconut milk, bay leaf, bruised whole lemongrass and salt. Make sure the rice is covered by 3cm of liquid. Bring to the boil, cover with a lid and simmer for 15 minutes or until the rice is tender and the liquid has been absorbed. Remove the bay and lemongrass, and serve.

450g basmati rice
30ml peanut oil
2 x 400g tins of coconut milk
1 bay leaf
2 stalks of lemongrass
5ml salt

Cucumber Relish with Toasted Rice

POUR the vinegar into a saucepan with the sugar, water and salt. Bring to the boil. Once the sugar has dissolved, remove the saucepan from the heat and cool.

IN a bowl combine the seeded and finely sliced cucumber, sliced red onion, finely sliced chilli discs and sesame seeds. When you are ready to serve, pour in the syrup, toss together well and transfer to a serving dish.

GARNISH with toasted rice and serve with your meal. For the toasted rice, cook 60ml of rice in a frying pan over low heat until just starting to colour. This will take about 30 minutes.

GRIND the cooled rice in a mortar and pestle or a coffee grinder. We use an electric coffee grinder for grinding our spices, peppercorns and sesame seeds.

45ml rice wine vinegar
45ml sugar
60ml water
pinch salt
1 English cucumber
1 red onion
1 long red chilli
15ml sesame seeds
15ml toasted rice

Stir-fried Green Beans & Sesame Seeds

MIX the soy sauce, sesame oil, sweet chilli sauce and black vinegar together and set aside.

HEAT a wok, heat the peanut oil and stir-fry the trimmed green beans for 5 minutes, pour in the soy sauce liquid and cook until thick. Tip the green beans onto a platter, garnish with black sesame seeds and serve.

15ml soy sauce
15ml sesame oil
45ml sweet chilli sauce
15ml black rice vinegar
30ml peanut oil
250g green beans
30ml black sesame seeds

Mint Ice Cream with Ginger Biscuits

POUR the cream and milk into a saucepan and bring to the boil. Whisk the vanilla, egg yolks and sugar until thick and pale in colour. Pour three-quarters of the cream onto the eggs and whisk until dissolved. Pour the egg mixture back into the saucepan and cook over low heat until the custard coats the back of a spoon, stirring constantly. Tip the bruised mint into a bowl, strain the custard onto the mint and cool.

Place in the fridge for 2 hours or overnight. Strain the mint custard and churn in an ice-cream machine. Serve the ice-cream sandwiched between 2 ginger nuts.

300ml cream
300ml milk
2ml vanilla extract
6 egg yolks
175g caster sugar
half a bunch mint
1 packet ginger nuts

Afternoon
Delights

Benedict Bars

FOR the base, dice the cold butter into a mixing bowl, sift the flour, corn flour and baking powder on top, then add the caster sugar, salt and orange extract.

RUB together gently between your fingertips and mix together until mixture forms a ball. You can add a little milk if it does not come together. Pre-heat the oven to 180°C. Grease a Swiss roll tin with butter and set aside.

FOR the topping, mix together the butter, caster sugar, vanilla extract, almonds and milk in a saucepan and melt over gentle heat, then set aside.

PRESS the shortbread dough into the base of three-quarters of the tin, spread a layer of jam over the surface, then spread the topping over the jam. Bake for 25–30 minutes or until set. Cool in the tin for 10 minutes and cut into rectangles.

Base

150g butter
225g cake flour
60ml corn flour
3ml baking powder
120g caster sugar
2ml sea salt
5ml orange extract

Topping

100g butter
60g caster sugar
5ml vanilla extract
200g flaked almonds
45–60ml milk
good-quality apricot jam

{ Makes 16 }

Vanilla Sponge Cake with Strawberries

PRE-HEAT the oven to 180°C. Line a 20cm spring-form cake tin with greaseproof paper. Lightly grease with butter and dust with flour. Sift the cake flour, corn flour and baking powder together and set aside. Whisk the egg whites until stiff, lightly whisk in the caster sugar. To the whisked egg whites stir in the beaten egg yolks, sifted cake-flour mixture and vanilla until just combined.

SCRAPE into the cake tin, level the surface with a spatula and bake for 25–30 minutes or until a skewer inserted into the cake comes away clean. Cool in the tin for 10 minutes.

WHISK the cream to soft peaks, stir in the crème fraîche and set aside. Once the cake has cooled, cut in half, place the base of the cake onto a plate, top with the crème fraîche, cream and sliced strawberries.

LIGHTLY press down the second sponge, dust with icing sugar and serve. This cake is best eaten on the day that it's made.

Sponge

50g cake flour
45ml cornflour
7ml baking powder
4 eggs
175g caster sugar
5ml vanilla bean paste

Filling

200ml cream
200g crème fraîche
250g strawberries

{ Serves 10 }

Syrupy Orange Cake with Ganache

PRE-HEAT the oven to 180°C. Line a 26cm spring-form cake tin with greaseproof paper, lightly grease the tin and dust with cake flour. Cream the butter, sugar and orange extract until pale in colour, slowly beat in the eggs. Fold in the sifted flour, orange juice and flour.

SCRAPE into the cake tin and bake for 45–60 minutes or until a skewer comes away clean when inserted into the cake. For the orange syrup, tip the orange juice, sugar and water in a saucepan and bring to the boil and simmer for a couple of minutes. Once the cake comes out of the oven, pour the syrup over and cool.

FOR the ganache, heat the chopped chocolate and cream together in the microwave for 3 minutes, whisk until smooth, then add the cold chopped butter and whisk until dissolved, set aside for 2 hours before using or overnight in a cool place. Spread the ganache around the sides and top of the cooled cake.

350g butter
330g caster sugar
20ml orange extract
6 eggs
350g self-raising flour
60ml orange juice

Orange Syrup
100ml orange juice
85g caster sugar
30ml water

Ganache
150g dark chocolate
100ml cream
50g butter

{ Serves 8 }

Chocolate Pecan Nut Cake

PRE-HEAT the oven to 180°C. Line a 26cm spring-form cake tin with greaseproof paper, lightly grease the tin and dust with cake flour. Melt the chocolate and butter in the microwave for 4 minutes or until melted.

WHISK the egg whites with one-third of the sugar until firm peaks form. Set aside. Whisk the egg yolks and remaining of the sugar until pale and double in volume. Fold the melted chocolate into the whisked egg yolks, then the sifted flour, ground pecan nuts and lastly fold in the whisked egg whites.

SCRAPE the batter into the cake tin and bake for 50–60 minutes or until a skewer comes away clean when inserted into the cake. Cool in the tin for 10 minutes.

SPREAD the ganache on top of the cooled cake and garnish with strawberries. Place the cake onto a plate and serve.

Cake
180g 70% dark chocolate
180g butter
4 eggs
140g caster sugar
200g pecan nuts
100g cake flour

To Serve
ganache
125g strawberries

Ginger Cheesecake

PRE-HEAT the oven to 170°C. Line a 20cm spring-form cake tin with greaseproof paper. Grind the ginger nuts in a food processor until fine and stir with the melted butter, press into the prepared cake tin and set aside.

WHISK the cream cheese, potato flour, eggs, vanilla and caster sugar until smooth, lightly whisk in half the sour cream and the chopped ginger. Scrape into the cake tin, bake in a bain-marie for 35–40 minutes. The cake should wobble slightly in the centre when carefully shaken. Spread over the remaining sour cream and bake for a further 10 minutes.

REMOVE the ginger cheesecake from the bain-marie and cool. Place the cake onto a plate, remove the spring-form sides of the tin, dust with icing sugar and serve.

300g ginger nuts
60g butter
600g smooth cream cheese
20ml potato flour
2 eggs
5ml vanilla extract
100g caster sugar
280g sour cream
2 knobs stem ginger
icing sugar

{ Serves 8 }

Apple, Raisin & Cream Cheese Cake

PRE-HEAT the oven to 180°C. Line a 20cm spring-form cake tin with greaseproof paper. Lightly grease with butter and dust with flour. Whisk together the sugar, cream cheese, softened butter and vanilla until smooth. Whisk in the eggs one at a time until well incorporated. Sift the flour and baking powder over the cream cheese mixture, tip in the raisins and mix until well combined. Scrape into the cake tin, top with the peeled and sliced apples, sprinkle extra caster sugar over and bake for 45–60 minutes or when a skewer inserted into the cake comes away clean. Cool in the tin for 10 minutes.

PLACE the cake onto a plate, remove the spring-form sides of the tin, and dust with icing sugar and serve. For individual cakes, spoon the sponge into 18 muffin tin cups.

450g caster sugar
450g smooth cream cheese
175g butter
5ml vanilla bean paste
3 eggs
300g cake flour
12ml baking powder
100g raisins
5 apples

{ Serves 8 }

Walnut Tart

FOR the sweet pastry, tip the flour, chopped butter and caster sugar into a large mixing bowl. Rub the butter between your fingers until the mixture resembles fine breadcrumbs.

LIGHTLY whisk the egg and iced water together, add to the flour mixture. You may not need all the liquid or you may need to add more. Stir until the dough comes together. Tip the dough onto a lightly floured surface and bring the it together to form a flattish ball. Wrap in clingfilm and place in the fridge for an hour.

PRE-HEAT the oven to 180°C. Roll out the pastry on a lightly floured surface to line a 30cm tart tin and prick the base of the tart with a fork. Place in the fridge for 10 minutes. Bake blind for 15 minutes or until cooked. Spread the jam over the base of the tart.

CREAM the butter and sugar together until pale in colour and slowly beat in the eggs one at a time. Add the vanilla and then the ground walnuts and cake flour. Spread over the base of the tart, making sure that you have distributed the filling evenly.

BAKE for 45 minutes or until the filling is set. Remove the tart from the tin and dust with icing sugar. This tart is always best the day after baking.

Sweet Pastry

250g cake flour
125g butter
15ml caster sugar
1 egg
40ml iced water

Filling

100ml youngberry jam
300g caster sugar
300g butter
4 eggs
10ml vanilla
300g walnuts
70g cake flour

{ Serves 10 }

{ Night Menus }

China Doll

Cosy Sunday Dinner

Pip's Pork Pie

Vegetarian Dinner Party

No Fuss Entertaining

Budget Cuts

Cold Christmas Buffet

Pot Roast & Potatoes

Colonial Portuguese

One Night in Bangkok

Vegetarian Buffet

Winter Curries

China Doll

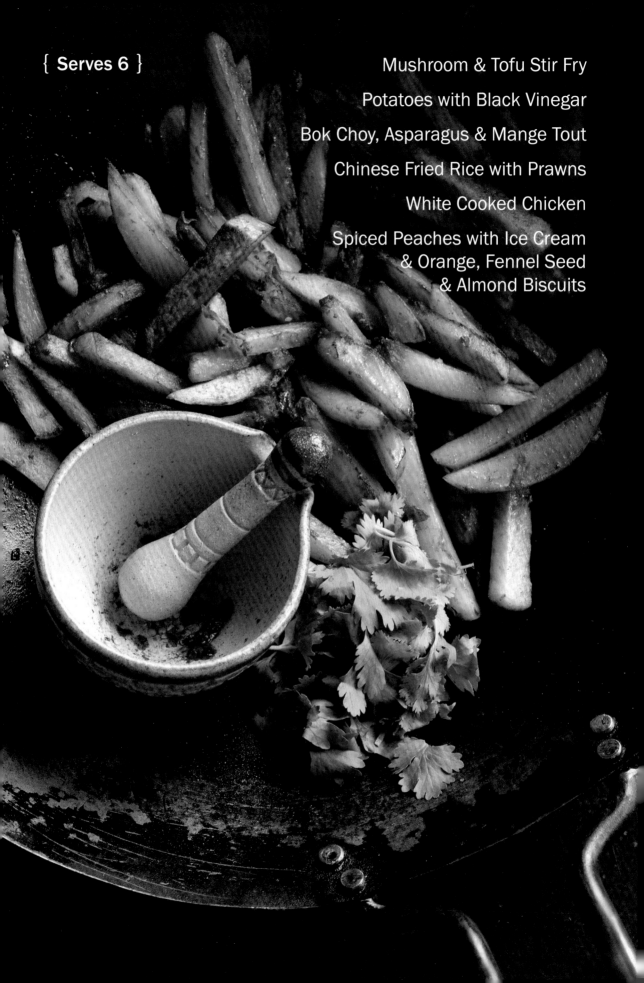

Mushroom & Tofu Stir Fry

LIGHTLY whisk the chicken stock, oyster sauce and soy together and set aside. Heat the peanut oil in a wok until smoking.

SEAL the cubed and drained tofu in the hot oil for 4–5 minutes until lightly golden in colour and set aside. In the hot wok fry the shredded spring onion, crushed garlic, sliced mushrooms and stir-fry for 2 minutes.

POUR in the chicken stock liquid and cook for 2 minutes. Carefully stir in the tofu and arrange on a serving platter.

70ml chicken stock
45ml oyster sauce
40ml soy sauce
70ml peanut oil
300g firm tofu
1 bunch spring onion
1 garlic clove
200g button mushrooms
200g oyster mushrooms
250g baby button mushrooms

Potatoes with Black Vinegar

BLANCH the matchstick-cut potatoes in salted water for 5 minutes, drain and dry well. Heat the wok until smoking, add the oil and the potatoes, and stir-fry for 10 minutes. They will start to crisp up in the hot oil.

ADD the rice vinegar, soy sauce and salt, and cook until the liquid has been absorbed. Garnish with chopped coriander and sprinkle over the dried chilli.

900g baking potatoes
70ml peanut oil
45ml black rice vinegar
45ml soy sauce
5ml salt
10g coriander
3ml crushed dried chilli

Bok Choy, Asparagus & Mange Tout

HEAT the wok and pour in the peanut oil and quickly fry the quartered bok choy, sliced asparagus, mange tout and sliced ginger. Stir-fry for 2 minutes, then pour in the shao hsing wine, sugar, soy sauce, sesame oil, water and vinegar.

ONCE thick, add the mint and coriander leaves and serve.

60ml peanut oil
2 bok choy
1 bunch asparagus
1 punnet mange tout
5cm knob ginger
30ml shao hsing wine
5ml sugar
30ml light soy sauce
5ml sesame oil
60ml water
5ml black vinegar
10g mint
10g coriander

Chinese Fried Rice with Prawns

HEAT the oil in a wok until smoking, pour in the beaten egg and lightly scramble the eggs with chopsticks and cook for a minute until the base is crispy and the egg is cooked. Carefully remove the scrambled egg from the wok.

IN the hot wok, fry the sliced onion, shredded ginger and chopped bacon. Once cooked, tip in the prawns and stir-fry for 2 minutes. Pour in the shao hsing wine, sugar and cooked rice. Stir the rice and cook until the rice is heated through.

ADD the scrambled eggs, light soy, oyster sauce, sesame oil and shredded spring onion. Check the seasoning, arrange on a platter and garnish with coriander leaves.

40ml sunflower oil
3 eggs
1 onion
5cm knob ginger
100g streaky bacon
250g peeled prawns
15ml shao hsing wine
5ml sugar
500ml cooked rice
40ml light soy sauce
30ml oyster sauce
10ml sesame oil
half a bunch spring onion
10g coriander

White Cooked Chicken

PLACE the water, shao hsing wine, light soy sauce, chopped onion, chopped carrot, orange peel, whole garlic, shards of ginger, salt and yellow rock sugar in a large pot. Bring to the boil and lay the chicken in the hot stock, breast side down and simmer gently for 30 minutes. Remove the pot from the heat and set aside for 3 hours. Gently remove the chicken from the stock and cut into pieces and arrange on a platter.

MIX the sesame oil, soy, caster sugar and black pepper in a mixing bowl. When you are ready to heat, pour the sesame liquid over the chicken. Heat the peanut oil in a saucepan, then over the chicken, and garnish with the coriander leaves and shredded chilli.

4L water
250ml shao hsing wine
250ml light soy sauce
1 onions
1 carrot
1 orange
6 garlic cloves
2 x 5cm knobs ginger
60ml sea salt
100g yellow rock sugar (2 blocks)
1.6kg whole chicken
30ml sesame oil
45ml soy sauce
5ml caster sugar
2ml black pepper
10g coriander
2 red chilli
60ml peanut oil

Spiced Peaches

TIP the sugar in a saucepan with the cinnamon stick, star anise, crushed cardamom pods, fennel seeds, peppercorns, lemon juice and a litre of water. Bring to the boil, then add the peaches and simmer for 30 minutes, or until the fruit is soft.

REMOVE the peaches from the syrup, reserving the syrup. When the peaches are cool enough to handle, peel and transfer to a serving bowl and pour in enough syrup to cover.

SERVE at room temperature with vanilla ice cream and orange, fennel seeds and almond biscuits. The remaining syrup will last for 3 months in the fridge; it is great for poaching pears or pineapple, and as a dressing on fresh fruit salad.

450g caster sugar
1 cinnamon stick
1 star anise
3 cardamom pod
2 fennel seeds
6 Szechwan peppercorns
juice of half a lemon
4 ripe peaches
vanilla ice cream (page 94)

Orange, Fennel Seed & Almond Biscuits

CREAM the softened butter, sugar, fennel seeds and orange zest together in an electric mixer until pale in colour. Beat in the eggs one at a time until well incorporated. On low speed, slowly add the sifted cake flour and baking powder until the dough starts to form a ball. Add the ground almonds. Scrape the dough into a bowl and place in the fridge for 30 minutes.

TIP the dough onto a lightly floured work surface, divide the dough into 2, roll each ball into a sausage shape about 12cm in length, wrap in clingfilm and place in the fridge for an hour or overnight in the fridge.

PRE-HEAT the oven to 180°C. Slice the logs into 2cm discs, lay on a greased baking tray and bake for 10–12 minutes or until light brown in colour. Cool on a wire rack and continue to cook the remaining dough.

80g butter
170g caster sugar
2ml fennel seeds
zest of half an orange
2 eggs
250g cake flour
5ml baking powder
80g ground almonds

{ Makes about 40 }

—

Cosy Sunday Dinner

{ Serves 8 }

Roasted Cumin
& Orange Olives

Cauliflower Soup with Gorgonzola,
Raisin & Pine Nut Relish

Braised Oxtail with Pesto Dumplings

Butternut & Spinach Gratin with Ricotta Custard

Banana & Chilli Tatin with
Vanilla Ice Cream

Roasted Cumin Seed & Orange Olives

PRE-HEAT the oven to 200°C. Toast the cumin and fennel seeds in a dry frying pan and heat until fragrant, tip into a mortar and pestle and lightly pound. Tip the seeds into a bowl and stir in the crushed garlic, orange zest, olives, sun-dried tomatoes and olive oil, and toss together.

TRANSFER to a roasting tray and roast for 15–20 minutes or until the olives begin to wrinkle slightly. Remove from oven, add balsamic vinegar and chopped parsley, season to taste with freshly ground black pepper, and mix well.

SERVE the olives warm or at room temperature. You will have more olives than you need. Store in the fridge for up to 6 weeks or bottle and give to your friends as a gift.

30ml cumin seeds
30ml fennel seeds
2 garlic cloves
zest of 1 orange
200g garlic-stuffed green olives
200g kalamata olives
200g large Egyptian black olives
200g sun-dried tomatoes
60ml olive oil
10ml balsamic vinegar
10g Italian parsley leaves

{ Makes 5 cups }

Cauliflower Soup with Gorgonzola, Raisin & Pine Nut Relish

PLACE the raisins in a bowl, cover with boiling water and set aside for 5 minutes to soften slightly. Melt the butter in a saucepan and tip in the drained raisins, vinegar, sugar, thyme leaves, cinnamon and pine nuts.

BRING to the boil and cook on medium heat for 10 minutes. Remove from the heat, cool and stir in the peeled, cored and finely chopped apples, then season with salt and pepper.

MELT the butter for the soup in a large saucepan and fry the sliced onions until soft. Add the chopped cauliflower, thyme and bay leaves and season with salt and pepper. Pour in the chicken stock, stir and bring to a simmer. Then cover and simmer for 20 minutes or so, until the cauliflower is very soft.

CRUMBLE in the gorgonzola and stir until it has melted into the soup, then stir in the crème fraîche. Pick out the bay leaves, then blend until really smooth. Reheat gently and check the seasoning.

LADLE into warm soup plates and spoon a little relish into the centre. Garnish with chopped parsley.

Raisin & Pine Nut Relish
90ml raisins
50g butter
150ml red wine vinegar
60ml caster sugar
3 sprigs thyme
1 cinnamon stick
60ml pine nuts
6 apples

Soup
30g butter
2 medium cauliflowers
4 onions
8 sprigs thyme
4 bay leaves
salt and black pepper
2 litres chicken stock
250g gorgonzola/blue cheese
200ml crème fraîche
Italian parsley

Braised Oxtail with Pesto Dumplings

PRE-HEAT oven to 160°C. Season the flour with salt and pepper, then toss the oxtail pieces oxtail to coat evenly. Heat the oil in a large saucepan and work in batches to seal the oxtail, browning the meat well on all sides. Leave the juices in the pan and fry the sliced onion, chopped carrot, chopped celery and sliced garlic, until it just starts to colour. Stir in the tomato purée and herbs, tip the meat back into the pan, pour over the wine, season with salt and pepper, and pour in enough water to cover the meat.

COVER the pan with a lid and cook in the oven for 3 hours until the meat is tender. You may need to add a little extra water during the cooking process.

BLITZ the flour, pesto and butter in a food processor with a generous pinch of salt until it's the texture of breadcrumbs. Gradually add the egg whites and blitz until everything comes together. On a floured surface, roll the dumplings into walnut-size balls. Bring a large pan of salted water to the boil, simmer dumplings for 10 minutes, then remove with a slotted spoon. Add the dumplings to the oxtail and serve.

30ml plain flour
1500g oxtails
60ml sunflower oil
2 onions
3 carrots
2 celery sticks
2 garlic cloves
30ml tomato purée
2 bay leaves
2 sprigs of rosemary
400ml red wine
salt and black pepper

Dumplings
300g self-raising flour
60ml homemade pesto
75g butter
3 egg whites

Butternut & Spinach Gratin with Ricotta Custard

PRE-HEAT the oven to 180°C. Blanch the spinach in salted water until tender, then drain and refresh in iced water. Heat the oil in a saucepan and add the thinly sliced leeks, crushed garlic and bay leaf, season with salt and pepper and cook for 2 minutes.

ADD the cubed butternut and water and cook for a further 15–20 minutes or until the butternut is soft but still holding its shape. Discard the bay leaf and transfer to an ovenproof dish. Melt the butter in a frying pan, reheat the spinach in the hot butter for 1–2 minutes and season with salt, pepper and nutmeg to taste.

SPOON the vegetables in the dish. To make the custard, whisk the cream cheese, eggs and grated Parmesan cheese together in a bowl, pour over the vegetables and top with a little more grated nutmeg, then bake for 20 minutes or until the custard has risen and is golden-brown. Leave to stand in a warm place for 10 minutes before serving.

900g spinach
15ml olive oil
1 leek
1 clove of garlic
1 bay leaf
salt and black pepper
300g peeled butternut
100ml water
30g butter
freshly grated nutmeg

Custard
225g cream cheese
2 eggs
50g Parmesan cheese

Banana & Chilli Tatin

PRE-HEAT the oven to 200°C. On medium heat, melt the butter and sugar in a medium frying pan that is able to go into the oven. Slice the bananas into 4. Once the sugar and butter mixture has turned a caramel colour, remove from the heat.

SCATTER the sliced chillies and cardamom seeds over the caramel and stir. Place the bananas on top cut-side down. Roll the pastry lightly and cut a circle 2cm bigger than the frying pan. Place the pastry on top of the bananas, tuck the edges down the side of the pan; prick the pastry a couple of times with a fork.

BAKE for 30 minutes or until the pastry is golden in colour. Remove from the oven and cool for 10 minutes. Place a dinner plate on top of the tatin. Carefully invert the pan; you may need to help loosen the bananas from the pan. Serve with vanilla bean ice-cream.

60ml butter
120g caster sugar
6 bananas
2 red chillies
4 cardamom pods
250g puff pastry
vanilla ice cream (page 94)

Pip's Pork Pie

{ **Serves 4** }

Pork & Date Pie

Tomato & Almond Preserve

Pickled Spiced Beetroot

Brinjal & Mozzarella Rolls

Pork & Date Pie

MELT the butter in a pan and fry the chopped onion until soft, stir in the chopped sage, chopped rosemary, mace, mustard powder and mixed spice, and set aside. Once the onions are cool, stir in the finely chopped pork, chopped dates, salt and pepper. Place the bowl in the fridge while you make the pastry. Pre-heat the oven to 200°C. Grease a 16cm square spring-form cake tin with butter and flour.

FOR the pastry, melt the water and the Holsum together and bring to the boil. Sift the flour and salt into a large mixing bowl, leaving a well in the centre. Pour in the boiling water and stir in the flour to form a dough. Knead lightly by hand to give you a smooth dough. Be careful, the pastry will be quite warm.

ROLL three-quarters of the dough out to fit the base and the sides of the tin with a 3cm overhang. Fill the mould with the pork filling, packing it in just above the top of the mould. Fold the pastry around the top onto the mix and brush with beaten egg. Roll out the remaining pastry to form a lid, pressing the edges together and cutting off any excess. Cut a hole in the middle of the pie, brush with beaten egg, sprinkle with sea salt.

PLACE the pie on a baking tray and bake for 20 minutes. Turn the oven down to 180°C and cook for 1½ hours. Remove the pie from the oven and cool for 30 minutes. Place a funnel in the pie hole and pour in 300ml of jellied stock, set aside for 30 minutes, then add the remaining jellied stock. You may not need all the jellied stock, pour in enough to fill the pie. To make the jellied stock, reduce 1½ litres of fresh chicken stock down to 600ml.

25g butter
2 onions
2 sprigs sage
2 sprigs rosemary
5ml ground mace
2ml English mustard powder
2ml mixed spice
600g pork belly
80g dates
salt and black pepper
600ml jellied stock

Pastry

600ml water
100g Holsum
450g cake flour
2ml salt

Tomato & Almond Preserve

TIP the peeled and chopped tomatoes, sugar and salt into a saucepan, bring to the boil and cook on medium heat for 20 minutes, stirring occasionally until you have a jam-like consistency. Stir in the toasted and chopped almonds, cook for a further minute and allow to cool.

STORE in sterilised bottles. The preserve is great served with cold roasted meats or used as a dressing for sweet potatoes and brinjals.

800g ripe tomatoes
100g caster sugar
2ml salt
60g flaked almonds

{ Makes 225ml }

Pickled Spiced Beetroot

BOIL the beetroot until tender, drain, then peel and slice. Tip into a bowl, add the raisins and set aside.

DRY-ROAST the fennel seeds and grind to a fine powder. Pour the vinegar into a saucepan and add the ground toasted fennel, sugar, ground cloves, ginger, peeled and sliced garlic, ground chilli, roughly ground pepper and salt. Bring the liquid to the boil and cook on medium heat for 45 minutes. The liquid must reduce by a third.

POUR the hot liquid over the beetroot and allow to cool. The pickled spiced beetroot will last up to 2 weeks in the fridge.

12 beetroot
100g raisins
2ml fennel seeds
700ml vinegar
150g brown sugar
6 whole cloves
15ml ground ginger
6 garlic cloves
1 bird's eye chilli
2ml ground black pepper
10ml sea salt

Brinjal & Mozzarella Rolls

SLICE the brinjals lengthways into 3mm slices and set aside. You should get 12 slices out of both brinjals. Pre-heat the oven to 180ºC. Shallow-fry the brinjals in olive oil for about 3 minutes on each side until golden and cooked through. Transfer to a plate lined with paper towel to absorb the excess oil.

TOP each brinjal slice with half a piece of ham, a slice of smoked mozzarella, and a blanched asparagus spear. Roll up along the longest side of the brinjal.

LAY the rolls in an oven dish, stir the breadcrumbs and the pesto together, and sprinkle over the brinjals. Bake for 5 minutes to heat through or until the mozzarella starts to melt. Serve warm.

2 large brinjals
olive oil for frying
120g thinly sliced ham
200g smoked mozzarella
12 asparagus spears
100g breadcrumbs
45ml homemade pesto

Fresh Chicken Stock

HEAT a large saucepan and fry the chopped onion, chopped celery and chopped leek in the butter until soft. Add the garlic, bay leaf, peppercorns, thyme, chopped chicken bones and pour in the water. Bring the stock to the boil and cook on medium heat for an hour.

STRAIN through a sieve and set aside to cool. Store any left-over stock in 250ml tubs and keep in the freezer until needed. Great for gravy, soups and quick sauces.

2 onions
2 celery sticks
2 leeks
25g butter
1 garlic clove
1 bay leaf
3 black peppercorns
1 sprig thyme
1.8kg chicken bones
3.5L water

{ Makes 2 litres }

Vegetarian
Dinner Party

Cream Cheese, Carrot & Truffle Tartlets

Beetroot Mousse with Lentil Vinaigrette

Mushroom & Almond Pâté en Croute
with Cranberry & Orange Sauce

Grilled Baby Vegetables with Pesto

Crushed Potatoes with White Wine,
Cherry Tomatoes & Herbs

Crimson Raisin & Walnut Cake

{ **Serves 8** }

Cream Cheese, Carrot & Truffle Tartlets

PRE-HEAT the oven to 180°C. Roll out the pastry and cut out discs with a 5cm cutter, line the mini muffin tins, bake blind and set aside. A great tip to bake the mini tartlets is to line the base with a mini cupcake cup lining and a spoonful of baking beans.

TIP the small-diced carrot into a saucepan with the maple syrup and balsamic vinegar and cook over low heat until tender and starting to caramelise, then set aside to cool.

STIR together the cream cheese, snipped chives, salt and pepper. Fill the cooled tart cases with a spoon of cream cheese filling, then top with a spoon of carrots, drizzle over a little truffle oil, and serve.

250g ready-made short crust pastry
4 carrots
60ml maple syrup
15ml balsamic vinegar
125g smooth cream cheese
5g chives
salt and black pepper
10ml truffle oil

{ **Makes 24 mini tartlets** }

Beetroot Mousse with Lentil Vinaigrette

FOR the lentil vinaigrette, place the lentils in a saucepan, cover with water and cook on medium heat until tender (about 20 minutes), then drain.

WHISK together the crushed garlic, mustard, vinegar, olive oil, salt and pepper. Stir in the finely chopped onion and drained lentils. Pre-heat the oven to 180°C, grease 8 ramekins with butter, and dust with extra breadcrumbs and set aside.

MIX the cooked, grated beetroot and Spanish spice together, then add the beaten eggs, beaten egg yolks, breadcrumbs, milk, cream, salt and pepper, and mix together. Pour into the pre-pared ramekins, place in a bain-marie and cook for 15 minutes or until the centre is set.

REMOVE from the oven and allow to cool, then unmould and set aside. When you are ready to serve, toss the baby spinach and the micro greens with a couple of spoons of lentil vinaigrette, divide the salad onto 8 plates, top with a beetroot mousse and spoon over the remaining lentil vinaigrette.

Lentil Vinaigrette

150g Puy lentils
2 garlic cloves
10ml Dijon mustard
30ml sherry vinegar
180ml olive oil
quarter red onion
120g baby spinach
50g micro greens/ watercress

Mousse

400g beetroot
30ml 'NoMU' Spanish spice
4 eggs
2 egg yolks
160g breadcrumbs
380ml milk
110ml cream
salt and black pepper

Mushroom & Almond Pâté en Croute with Cranberry & Orange Sauce

PRE-HEAT the oven to 200°C. Place the butter in a saucepan with the chopped onion, crushed garlic, sliced celery, paprika, chopped thyme leaves and chopped rosemary. Cook until just soft. Stir in the sliced mushrooms, soy sauce and lemon juice. Cook until all the liquid has evaporated.

REMOVE from the heat and stir in the almonds and sliced spring onions so that the pâté en croute is a fairly firm consistency. Season with salt and pepper.

ROLL out each defrosted pastry into a large rectangle. Place the half of the mushroom pâté in the middle of each pastry sheet in a long sausage shape. You can pile the pâté en croute up fairly high. With a sharp knife, cut out squares of pastry from each corner, cutting almost to the edge of the pâté en croute.

BRUSH the edges with a little of the beaten egg to ensure that the pastry stays together when cooked. Pull the shortest edges over the pâté en croute, then pull the long sides of the pastry over and pinch together forming an attractive ridge along the middle. Continue with the other puff pastry. Brush both with beaten egg and bake for 30 minutes or until golden brown.

FOR the sauce, place all the cranberries, orange juice, caster sugar and star anise together in a saucepan and cook until soft.

50g butter
2 onion
4 cloves garlic
4 sticks celery
15ml paprika
2 sprigs thyme
2 sprigs rosemary
250g portobellini mushrooms
200g oyster mushrooms
120g shiitake mushrooms
250g white button mushrooms
30ml soy sauce
juice of 1 lemon
100g ground almonds
50g toasted flaked almonds
1 bunch spring onions
2 x 250g rolls puff pastry
1 egg

Cranberry & Orange Sauce

450g fresh/frozen cranberries
juice of 2 oranges
120g caster sugar
1 star anise

Grilled Baby Vegetables with Pesto

STIR the baby corn, sliced baby gem, chopped baby marrow, halved butternuts, crushed garlic, rosemary oil, salt and pepper together in a mixing bowl.

PLACE on a smoking grill pan and grill until just charred. Tip into a bowl and stir in the pesto and chopped parsley, check the seasoning and serve on a platter.

1 punnet baby corn
1 punnet baby gems
1 baby marrow
1 punnet baby butternut
2 garlic clove
rosemary olive oil
salt and black pepper
80ml homemade pesto
10g Italian parsley

Crushed Potatoes with White Wine, Cherry Tomatoes & Herbs

PLACE the potatoes in saucepan and cover with water, season well with salt and bring to the boil, then turn down to a simmer.

STIR the halved cherry tomatoes, olive oil, lemon juice and the white wine together in a mixing bowl and set aside. When the potatoes are cooked, drain the water. Add the butter and season with salt and pepper.

ROUGHLY crush the potatoes with a wooden spoon, add the marinating tomatoes, chopped spring onion, chopped parsley, torn basil and chopped rocket.

600g new potatoes
salt and black pepper
250g cherry tomatoes
80ml olive oil
juice of half a lemon
250ml white wine
45ml soft butter
6 spring onions
15g flat parsley
15g basil leaves
15g rocket

Crimson Raisin & Walnut Cake

PRE-HEAT the oven to 160°C. Line the base of a 26cm spring-form cake tin with greaseproof paper. Lightly grease with butter and dust with flour.

TIP the walnuts and raisins into a small saucepan and cover with cold water. Bring to the boil, then simmer for 10 minutes.

DRAIN in a colander, discarding the liquid, and return to the pan. Add the chopped butter to the pan and stir over a low heat until it has melted.

WHISK the eggs and sugar for 30 seconds in a large bowl, then stir in the walnut mixture and the whisky. Sift the flour and baking powder into the mixture and stir until well combined.

SPOON the cake mixture into the tin and bake it in the centre of the oven for 40–50 minutes or until an inserted skewer comes away clean. Cool in the tin for 10 minutes.

PLACE the cake on a plate. Spread the mascarpone over it and scatter on the hulled and halved strawberries, dust with icing sugar and serve.

100g walnut halves
125g crimson raisins
140g butter
200g brown sugar
2 eggs
50ml whisky
175g flour
8ml baking powder
200g mascarpone
250g strawberries

{ Serves 10 }

No Fuss
Entertaining

Calamari, Roast Butternut
& Chilli Salad

Quinoa, Olive & Tomato Salad with
Chopped Egg Dressing

Bulgar-stuffed Baby Marrow

Cold Roasted Fillet of Beef with
Green Peppercorn Béarnaise Sauce

Carrots with Honey, Ginger & Thyme

Berry & Cream Cheese Tartlets

{ Serves 8 }

Calamari, Roast Butternut & Chilli Salad

PRE-HEAT the oven to 180°C. Tip the peeled and cubed butternut onto a roasting tray, drizzle with a little of the peanut oil, soy sauce, salt, pepper and 90ml boiling water, and roast for 30 minutes or until tender.

BLANCH the scored calamari in salted boiling water for 40 seconds, tip into a colander and set aside. Heat a lightly oiled pan until the oil just starts to smoke and stir-fry the calamari until opaque and browning in places.

TIP the peanuts into a mortar and pestle and roughly grind, then transfer to a small bowl. Add the chopped chilli, peeled garlic, salt and sugar to the mortar and pestle, and smash and grind together to form a paste. Then stir in the fish sauce, sesame oil and juiced lime.

TASTE and adjust the seasoning and transfer the dressing to a large bowl and add the calamari and chopped coriander. Arrange the roasted butternut onto a large platter and scatter over the dressed calamari. Garnish with the peanuts and coriander leaves.

2 butternuts (800g)
90ml peanut oil
60ml soy sauce
salt and black pepper
400g calamari tubes
10g coriander

Dressing
100ml raw peanuts
2 red chillies
4 garlic cloves
45ml palm sugar
30ml Thai fish sauce
10ml sesame oil
15ml lime juice

Quinoa, Rocket, Olive & Tomato Salad with Chopped Egg Dressing

BOIL the quinoa in salted water for 20–30 minutes or until it begins to unwrap. Drain through a fine sieve to cool.

FRY the halved tomatoes for a couple of minutes on each side in the olive oil, season with salt and pepper. You still want the tomatoes to retain a crunch. Add the olives to the pan. Remove the pan from the heat and lay the tomatoes onto a platter, scatter over the torn basil leaves and top with rocket.

FOR the dressing, cook the eggs in boiling water for 5 minutes, then drain and place in a bowl of iced water to cool them completely. Shell the eggs, then cut into quarters and set aside. Whisk together the chopped parsley, capers, olive oil, sherry vinegar, salt and pepper, and stir into the quinoa with the olives. Top the tomatoes with the quinoa and then the eggs, then season with salt and pepper to serve.

180ml quinoa
60–75ml olive oil
6 tomatoes
salt and black pepper
12 kalamata olives
5g basil
100g rocket

Dressing
4 eggs
10g Italian parsley
30ml capers
30ml olive oil
30 ml sherry vinegar

Bulgar-stuffed Baby Marrow

PRE-HEAT the oven to 180°C and grease a medium baking dish with oregano olive oil. Slice the baby marrow lengthwise, and remove the seeds to form boat-shaped containers. Put the baby marrow shells in the prepared dish, drizzle with the olive oil and sprinkle with salt and pepper. Bake for 10–15 minutes until tender but still holding their shape.

FRY the chopped onion in olive oil, add the pine nuts, ground cinnamon, crushed dried chilli, salt and pepper, and cook for a further minute. Tip in the bulgar and 75ml boiling water. Bring to the boil, remove from heat, cover with a lid and set aside to cool slightly. Fluff the cracked wheat and stir in the chopped sun-dried tomatoes and chopped mint. When the baby marrow shells are tender, spoon in the filling, distributing it evenly.

TOP each marrow with crumbled blue cheese and drizzle with a little garlic olive oil. Bake for 10–15 minutes, until the filling is heated through, and serve.

15ml oregano olive oil
8 baby marrow
salt and black pepper
15ml olive oil
2 medium onions
60ml pine nuts
3ml ground cinnamon
2ml crushed dried chilli
100g bulgar wheat
4 sun-dried tomatoes in olive oil
5g mint leaves
60g blue cheese

Roasted Fillet of Beef with Green Peppercorn Béarnaise Sauce

PRE-HEAT the oven to 200°C. Heat a grill pan, season the fillet with the olive oil, thyme leaves, salt and lots of pepper. Grill until golden in colour on all sides and place in the oven for 10–15 minutes. Remove the fillet from the oven and rest for 5 minutes.

SLICE the fillet and arrange on a platter with the jug of béarnaise sauce on the side. For the béarnaise sauce, put chopped onion, vinegar, wine, tarragon sprigs and dried tarragon in a saucepan. Bring to the boil and cook until reduced to 15ml. Remove from the heat and cool slightly.

WHISK the egg yolks with 25ml water, strained onion and vinegar. Place the pan over very low heat or over a simmering bain-marie and continue to whisk until the sauce is thick. Do not boil or the eggs will scramble. Remove the sauce from the heat, continue to whisk and slowly add the melted butter in a thin, steady stream.

STIR in the chopped green peppercorns, check the seasoning and serve. You can make the béarnaise about an hour before using, but keep next to warm heat, on the side of the stove.

750kg beef fillet
30ml olive oil
3 sprigs thyme
salt and black pepper

Béarnaise

half an onion
30ml tarragon vinegar
30ml white wine
5ml dried tarragon
3 eggs
200g clarified butter
45ml green peppercorns in brine

Carrots with Honey, Ginger & Thyme

PEEL the carrots and cut them in half lengthways. Place in a saucepan and pour over enough cold water to just cover. Add the honey, shredded ginger, butter, thyme leaves and a generous pinch of salt.

PLACE over a medium heat and bring to the boil, then lower the heat to a simmer. Cook for 10–20 minutes or until the carrots are almost tender. Now turn the heat up to boil the liquid rapidly until reduced down to a shiny, sweet glaze. There should be 1–2 tablespoons of intensely flavoured cooking liquor coating the carrots.

POUR in the rice vinegar and check the seasoning. Cool slightly. Just before serving, scatter over the feta balls and finely chopped chives.

8 medium carrots
30ml honey
5cm knob ginger
50g butter
6 thyme sprigs
salt and black pepper
15ml rice vinegar
1 tub black pepper feta balls
10g chives

Berry & Cream Cheese Tartlets

SIFT the flour into a bowl, then add the almonds and icing sugar. Rub the chopped butter into the flour with your fingertips until it resembles breadcrumbs. Make a well in the centre, add the lightly beaten egg and mix with a flat-bladed knife, using a cutting action, until the mixture comes together in beads.

GATHER the dough and put onto a lightly floured surface. Press into a ball, cover with plastic wrap and refrigerate for 30 minutes. Grease a 22cm tart tin or 8 medium fluted tart tins. Roll out the pastry to fit the base and side of tin or tins. Press the pastry into the tin, trim the edges and prick the base with a fork. Place in the fridge for 30 minutes.

PRE-HEAT the oven to 180°C. Line the pastry with crumpled baking paper and spread with baking beads or rice. Bake for 8–10 minutes, then remove the paper and beads.

PROCESS the cream cheese, vanilla, eggs, sugar and cream in a food processor until smooth.

TIP the berries into the tart shell and pour over the filling and bake for 12–20 minutes, or until the filling is just set; the top should be soft but not too wobbly. Cool, dust with icing sugar and serve.

Pastry

185g stone-ground cake flour
95g ground almonds
40g icing sugar
125g unsalted butter
1 egg

Filling

300g cream cheese
7ml vanilla extract
3 eggs
240g caster sugar
187ml cream
200g frozen berries
icing sugar, to dust

{ makes **8 medium tarts** }

Budget Cuts

Sweetcorn Cakes

Asian Spaghetti Bolognaise

Roasted Chilli Sauce

Raspberry Rice Pudding

{ **Serves 4** }

Sweetcorn Cakes

BLANCH the corn in boiling salted water until tender, drain, cool and cut the corn kernels off the cob. Mix together the corn kernels, beaten egg, rice flour, Thai curry powder, fish sauce, chopped coriander and finely chopped chilli. Mix to form a thick paste. You may need a little extra rice flour to bring the mixture together.

HEAT the peanut oil in a shallow frying pan and fry spoonfuls of the corn-cake batter and cook for 3–4 minutes on each side or until golden brown. Drain on kitchen paper and continue to cook the remaining corn cakes.

FOR the dipping sauce, stir together the vinegar, palm sugar and fish sauce until the sugar has dissolved, add the chopped chilli, chopped roasted peanuts and sesame seeds. Serve the sweetcorn cakes on a platter with the dipping sauce on the side.

Sweetcorn Cakes

2 ears corn on the cob
half a beaten egg
80ml rice flour
15ml Thai curry powder (page 140)
2 spring onions
10ml fish sauce
10g coriander
1 red chilli
peanut oil to shallow-fry

Dipping Sauce

30ml rice wine vinegar
30ml palm sugar
10ml fish sauce
1 red chilli
45ml peanuts
10ml black sesame seeds

Asian Spaghetti Bolognaise

FRY half the chopped spring onion in the peanut oil until soft, add the pork mince and stir-fry for 10 minutes. Add the curry paste, crushed garlic, shredded ginger and chopped chilli. Pour in the coconut milk, chicken stock, fish sauce and soy sauce. Bring the sauce to the boil and cook on medium heat for 20–30 minutes until reduced.

JULIENNE the cucumber and set aside with the shredded spring onion, coriander leaves and mint leaves. For the chilli sauce, stir together the chopped chilli, fish sauce and soy sauce and set aside. Boil the egg noodles in salted water for 5 minutes or until tender, then drain.

DIVIDE the noodles into 4 bowls, spoon in the meat, top with the julienne cucumber salad and, just before eating, spoon over a teaspoon of the roasted chilli sauce. If you are not a chilli fan, season with fish sauce for the best Asian flavour.

half a bunch spring onions
30ml peanut oil
500g pork mince
40ml mussaman curry paste
1 garlic clove
5cm knob ginger
1 chilli
400g tin coconut milk
250ml chicken stock
15ml fish sauce
30ml soy sauce
1 English cucumber
10g coriander
4 sprigs mint
400g egg noodles

Roasted Chilli Sauce

HEAT the peanut oil in a frying pan and fry the sliced onions and sliced garlic until starting to caramelise, stir in the shrimp paste and fry for 2 minutes.

TIP the cooked onions into a blender, add the chopped chillies, tamarind and palm sugar, and purèe until smooth. Return the paste to the frying pan, bring to the boil and then simmer for 5 minutes or until the mixture is starting to thicken.

REMOVE the pan from the heat and stir in the fish sauce. Spoon into a sterilized jar. Store in the fridge until needed. Roasted chilli sauce is great served as a condiment, stir in mayonnaise, great with grilled meats. A great alternative if someone does not enjoy fresh chilli.

60ml peanut oil
4 onions
8 garlic cloves
5 ml shrimp paste
10 dried red chillies
60ml tamarind concentrate
100ml palm sugar
30ml fish sauce

Raspberry Rice Pudding

HEAT the milk until just starting to boil, stir in the rice, sugar, a pinch of freshly grated nutmeg, bruised lemongrass and coconut milk, and stir occasionally over low heat for 25–35 minutes or until thick.

SPOON into 4 bowls, dollop a generous amount of raspberry jam in the centre and 30ml of coconut milk. The rice pudding can be served warm or at room temperature.

450ml milk
75g arborio rice
30g caster sugar
a grating of whole nutmeg
2 lemongrass stalks
120ml coconut milk
raspberry jam
extra coconut milk to serve

Cold Christmas Buffet

{ Serves 10 }

Pork, Prune & Pistachio Terrine

Szechwan Brinjals with Water Chestnuts

Rice, Prawn & Lemon Salad

Brussels Sprouts
with Caper Vinaigrette & Feta Cheese

Braised Red Cabbage
with Green Fig Preserve

Glazed Gammon with Marmalade

Pork, Prune & Pistachio Terrine

MIX the Marsala wine, white wine, thyme leaves and bay leaf together, then stir in 2.5cm cubed pork steaks, 2cm cubed pork belly and chopped, cleaned chicken livers, and place in the fridge overnight.

LINE a terrine tin that is 24cm long, 9cm wide and 10cm deep with a lid with clingfilm. Remove the meat from the fridge and set aside for 30 minutes, to come to room temperature. Remove the bay leaf, stir in the egg, pistachio nuts, pitted prunes, nutmeg and a generous amount of salt and pepper, and set aside. Pre-heat the oven to 180°C.

SCRAPE the bacon rashers with the back of a knife to stretch them. Lay the bacon strips in the dish, overlapping each rasher and leaving extra length overhanging the edge. After the terrine has been filled with the marinating mixture, the ends of bacon should be folded over the top of the mixture to form a lid.

FRY the chicken livers in a hot frying pan in the oil and butter, season with a little salt and black pepper, fry for 30 seconds and set aside. Place half of the pork filling on the base of the terrine, then the chicken livers, and then the remaining filling, press the mixture down firmly with the palm of your hand and cover with the overlapping bacon. Place a sheet of tin foil on top, then the lid.

PLACE in a bain-marie of hot water with a dishcloth on the bottom and bake for an hour and 45 minutes. Remove from the oven and cool for 2 hours, then place in the fridge overnight. To serve, remove the lid and the foil, and invert onto a board. Peel away the clingfilm, slice into portions and serve.

FOR a finer texture in the pork meat, use a food processor to chop the meats, but be careful not to over-blend the meat and fill your bowl with a third of the meat mixture.

Marinade

50ml Marsala wine
100ml dry white wine
2 sprigs thyme leaves
1 bay leaf
500g pork steaks
500g pork belly
150g chicken livers

Terrine

1 egg
40g pistachio nuts
80g pitted prunes
2ml grated whole nutmeg
salt and freshly pepper
500g packets streaky bacon

Chicken Liver Filling

200g chicken livers
15ml sunflower oil
20g butter
salt and black pepper

Szechwan Brinjals with Water Chestnuts

CUT the brinjals in half, then into wedges. Heat the peanut oil in a wok and fry the brinjals in batches until coloured. Remove the coriander leaves from the stalks and tip the stems into a mortar and pestle, add the crushed garlic and sliced ginger, and pound to a paste.

FRY the pounded garlic and sliced onion until soft, tip in the brinjals, drained and halved water chestnuts, tamari, kecap manis, vinegar, shaoxing wine, chilli oil and sugar.

COOK the brinjals for 2 minutes, then add the toasted and ground Szechwan pepper and coriander leaves, and serve.

500g brinjals
45ml peanut oil
10g coriander
4 garlic cloves
5cm knob fresh ginger
1 onion
¼ tin water chestnuts
30ml tamari
30ml kecap manis
75ml rice wine vinegar
75ml shao hsing rice wine
15ml chilli oil
40–60ml caster sugar
5ml Szechwan peppercorns

Rice, Prawn & Lemon Salad

HEAT the olive oil in a saucepan, add the rice and finely chopped celery, and cook for a couple of minutes.

POUR in the stock, salt and pepper, bring to the boil, cover with a lid and simmer for 20 minutes or until the rice is tender and the liquid has been absorbed. Remove the saucepan from the heat, and tip into a bowl to cool.

LIGHTLY toast the raisins and pine nuts until coloured and tip into the rice with the lemon peel and juice, olive oil, blanched prawns and chopped parsley. Check the seasoning and serve.

80ml olive oil
300g arborio rice
2 celery sticks
650ml hot vegetable stock
salt and black pepper
40g crimson raisins
40g pine nuts
peel and juice of 1 lemon
60ml olive oil
20ml lemon olive oil
800g peeled prawns
20g Italian parsley

Brussels Sprouts with
Caper Vinaigrette & Feta Cheese

SCORE the base end of each Brussels sprout with a deep cross, which will allow the heat to get into the heart of this dense little vegetable. Blanch the Brussels sprouts in boiling salted water until tender, drain and refresh in iced water, drain and set aside.

LIGHTLY whisk the crushed garlic, red wine vinegar, olive oil, salt, pepper, snipped chives and capers together. When you are ready to serve, stir together the Brussels sprouts, vinaigrette and crumbled feta.

600g Brussels sprouts

Vinaigrette

1 garlic clove
15ml red wine vinegar
60ml olive oil
salt and black pepper
10g chives
50ml capers
125g Danish feta cheese

Braised Red Cabbage with Green Fig Preserve

HEAT the oil in a saucepan, tip in the peeled and finely sliced red onion and lightly crushed juniper berries, and cook until the onions are soft.

ADD the finely shredded cabbage and cook for 10 minutes, pour in the apple juice, halved figs, salt and pepper. Bring the cabbage to the boil and cook on medium heat until most of the liquid has evaporated.

30ml olive oil
2 red onions
5ml juniper berries
1 large red cabbage
300ml apple juice
6 preserved figs

Glazed Gammon with Marmalade

TO cook a gammon, place in a large saucepan with the bay leaves, rosemary, black peppercorns, cloves, chopped onion, chopped carrot, brown sugar, vinegar, sliced garlic and enough water to cover the gammon. Bring to the boil, then simmer until cooked, about an hour.

PRE-HEAT the oven to 190°C. Remove the gammon from the pot and let it rest for 30 minutes. Line a roasting tray with foil and brush it with oil and place the gammon on the tray.

STIR the marmalade, Dijon mustard, sugar and orange juice together and spoon over the gammon. Bake for 20–30 minutes or until it looks glossy and fantastic.

REST for 20 minutes and calve into slices. Kentucky ham is a pork neck that has been cured like a gammon.

1 Kentucky ham
2 bay leaves
1 sprig rosemary
4 sprig thyme
5ml black peppercorns
5ml cloves
1 onion
2 carrots
30ml soft-brown sugar
30ml vinegar
1 garlic clove

Glaze

45ml marmalade
15ml Dijon mustard
60ml dark brown sugar
75ml orange juice

Pot Roast & Potatoes

Butternut & Split Pea Soup

Quick & Easy Dinner Rolls

Pot Roast Spiced Chicken

Roasted Potatoes with Milk,
Rosemary & Garlic

Cumin Roast Peppers,
Tomatoes & Olives

Vanilla Custard & Pine Nut Tart

{ Serves 6 }

Butternut & Split Pea Soup

HEAT the oil in a large saucepan and fry the cubed bacon until it starts to colour. Add the chopped onion and continue to fry until the onion is soft. Stir in the coriander, allspice, a good grinding of pepper, split peas and stock.

BRING to the boil, skim the surface if necessary, and simmer, covered for 20 minutes, then tip in the peeled and cubed butternut, bring back to a simmer and cook until the butternut is soft, about 20–30 minutes.

BLEND the soup in a blender, season with salt and black pepper. If the soup is too thick, dilute it with a little water. Garnish with sliced spring onions.

25ml sunflower oil
150g smoked bacon
1 large onion
5ml ground coriander
2.5ml allspice
salt and black pepper
150g yellow split peas
3 litres chicken stock
800g butternut
3 spring onions

Quick & Easy Dinner Rolls

PRE-HEAT the oven to 180°C. Mix the cake flour, whole-wheat flour, salt and sifted bicarbonate of soda in a mixing bowl.

STIR the flours together, make a well in the centre, then use a knife to stir in the buttermilk. Stir from the centre to the edge of the bowl in circles. You should have a dough that is soft but not sticky. You may need to add extra liquid if the dough is not coming together.

TIP the dough onto a lightly floured work surface and divide into 12 equal pieces. Lightly roll each into a ball. Transfer to a greased baking tray, brush the rolls with a little milk and sprinkle over the seeds, alternating between sesame and blue poppy.

BAKE for 10–20 minutes. The rolls should be golden in colour. Transfer to a wire rack and cool.

125g cake flour
125g whole-wheat flour
2.5ml sea salt
3ml bicarbonate of soda
250ml buttermilk
30ml sesame seeds
30ml blue poppy seeds

{ Makes 12 dinner rolls }

Pot Roast Spiced Chicken

PLACE the sliced onion, chopped ginger, sliced lemongrass stalks (the white part only), chopped coriander, 15ml oil and salt into a food processor and blitz to a paste.

WORK your fingers under the skin of the bird, carefully lifting it from the flesh without tearing it. Spread the spice mixture over the legs and breast, and draw the skin back in place. When you are a ready to cook, pre-heat the oven to 190°C.

HEAT the remaining oil in a heavy ovenproof casserole that is just big enough to take the chicken. Put in the lime leaves, place the chicken on its side on top of them and pour over the lime juice. Cover tightly with foil under the lid and transfer the pan to the oven. Bake for 30 minutes, turn the chicken over and cook for a further 30 minutes. Remove the lid, turn the chicken breast upwards and bake for 10–15 minutes more. Pierce the thickest part of the thigh with a skewer; if the juices run clear, the chicken is cooked.

REST it for 10 minutes in a warm place before carving. Discard the lime leaves and serve the chicken with the pan juices spooned over.

1 onion
60g ginger
3 stalks lemongrass
15g coriander leaves
45ml sunflower oil
salt and black pepper
1.8kg chicken
6 Thai lime leaves
60ml fresh lime juice

Roasted Potatoes with Milk, Rosemary & Garlic

IN a bowl large enough to hold all the ingredients, combine the milk, roughly chopped rosemary and sliced garlic, then set aside for 20 minutes. Pre-heat the oven to 200°C and grease a baking tray with a little olive oil.

CUT the potatoes into 5mm slices and add them to the bowl with the milk, season with salt and black pepper. Toss together well and tip the potatoes on a baking tray.

POUR over the milk mixture, bake in the oven for about 30 minutes, flipping the potatoes occasionally to make sure the slices brown evenly. Serve hot.

250ml milk
30ml rosemary leaves
4 garlic cloves
6 potatoes
salt and black pepper

Cumin Roast Peppers, Tomatoes & Olives

PRE-HEAT the oven to 190°C. Put the seeded and thickly sliced peppers into a shallow roasting dish and stir together with the olive oil, cherry tomatoes, cumin seeds, olives, salt and pepper.

ROAST for 30 minutes. Serve hot or at room temperature.

4 red peppers
45ml olive oil
500g cherry tomatoes
5ml cumin seed
100g fat green olives
salt and black pepper

Vanilla Custard & Pine Nut Tart

CREAM the butter and sugar until pale in colour. Beat in the sifted flour, lemon extract, egg and egg yolk until the dough comes together. Tip the dough onto a lightly floured surface and bring the dough together to form a flattish ball. Wrap in clingfilm and place in the fridge for an hour.

PRE-HEAT the oven to 180°C. Roll out two thirds of the pastry on a lightly floured surface to line a 30cm tart tin and prick the base of the tart with a fork. Place in the fridge for 10 minutes. Reserve the remaining pastry in the fridge for the top of the tart.

WHISK the egg yolks in a bowl with the sugar until pale and creamy. Stir the sifted flour into the egg mixture. Pour the milk into a saucepan with the vanilla paste and bring to the boil. Just before the milk comes to the boil, remove it from the heat and pour three-quarters of the milk onto the egg mixture, whisking until smooth. Pour the egg mixture back into the saucepan with the rest of the milk and cook on medium heat, stirring constantly until thick and you can't taste any flour.

REMOVE the saucepan from the heat and stir in the butter, scrape the custard into a bowl. Dust with icing sugar as this prevents a skin forming. Set aside to cool.

ASSEMBLE the tart by scraping the custard into the tart shell. Roll out the remaining pastry to make a disc to cover the top of the tart. Seal the pastry around the edge, brush with milk and sprinkle the pine nuts. Bake at 180°C for about 40 minutes until the top is golden. Cool for 2 hours before cutting.

Pastry

125g butter
125g caster sugar
250g cake flour
5ml lemon extract
1 egg
1 egg yolk

Custard

4 egg yolks
250g caster sugar
60g plain flour
500ml milk
3ml vanilla bean paste
20ml butter
30ml milk
30ml pine nuts

Colonial
Portuguese

Polenta Bread

Prawns with Chorizo,
White Wine & Peas

Poor Man's Potatoes

Chicken Flattie

Peri Peri Style Sauce

Crème Caramel

{ Serves 4 }

Polenta Bread

SIFT the flour and salt into bowl and stir in the polenta. Dissolve the yeast and sugar in 200ml of lukewarm water and sprinkle with a spoonful of flour. Work the yeasty liquid into the flour, adding as much of the water as you need to make a soft, sticky, rather wet dough.

TIP the dough out onto a lightly floured work surface and knead for 5 minutes, or until smooth. Transfer to a lightly oiled bowl, cover with clingfilm and set aside for an hour until more than doubled in volume. Knock back the dough, cut the dough into 10 balls and roll each ball into torpedo shapes. Sprinkle with extra polenta. Transfer to a greased baking tray, cover with a cloth and leave to rise again for 30 minutes.

PRE-HEAT the oven to 200°C. Bake the bread for about 20 minutes or until tapping produces a hollow sound. Cool on a wire rack. The bread freezes really well as the recipe makes 10 breads. Great made into one large loaf.

400g white bread flour
3ml salt
200g polenta
50g active dried yeast
5ml caster sugar
600ml warm water

{ Makes 10 rolls }

Prawns with Chorizo, White Wine & Peas

HEAT the olive oil and fry the sliced onion until soft. Add the chopped chorizo and cook for 5 minutes or until the chorizo is starting to colour.

ADD the de-veined prawns, crushed garlic, salt, pepper and white wine, and cover with a lid. Cook for 8–10 minutes or until the prawns are cooked, stir in the thawed peas, chopped parsley and serve with polenta bread.

60ml olive oil
1 large onion
110g chorizo
250g Mozambique prawns
2 garlic cloves
salt and black pepper
60ml white wine
250ml frozen peas
10g Italian parsley

Poor Man's Potatoes

HEAT the oil in a saucepan, add the peeled and sliced potatoes and salt, and cook for 10 minutes or until lightly golden in colour. Add the seeded and sliced green pepper, seeded and sliced red pepper, sliced onion and black pepper.

COVER with a lid and cook on low heat for 10 minutes. Stir in the chopped green pepper, sliced red onion and black pepper. Cover with a lid and cook for a further 20 minutes or until the potatoes are tender. Stir occasionally to prevent sticking.

200ml olive oil
4 baking potatoes
5ml salt
1 green pepper
1 red pepper
1 red onion
2ml black pepper

Chicken Flattie

IN a mortar and pestle pound the chopped chillies, sliced ginger and chopped garlic until you have a rough paste. Stir in the torn bay leaves, white wine, lemon juice, olive oil and black pepper.

TO score the chicken, cut on each side of the backbone using poultry shears, press down with the heel of your hand on the top of each breast to break the backbone and to flatten it. Cut deep slashes diagonally in each breast and on the legs. Rub the marinade onto the scored chicken and marinate in the fridge overnight or for a minimum of 3 hours.

PRE-HEAT the oven to 200°C. Transfer the chicken and the liquid to a baking tray, season with the sea salt and roast for 20 minutes, turn down the heat to 180°C and roast for a further 20–30 minutes or until the chicken is cooked through.

4 chillies
5cm knob ginger
4 garlic
3 bay leaves
100ml white wine
juice of 1 lemon
45ml olive oil
2ml black pepper
1.6kg chicken
15ml sea salt
5g Italian parsley

Peri-Peri Style Sauce

HEAT the olive oil, crushed chilli and chopped garlic for 2 minutes or until just starting to colour.

ADD the chopped tomatoes, chopped red pepper, sugar, salt and pepper, and cook for 20 minutes. Stir in the lemon juice and purée with a hand-blender until smooth.

BOTTLE into jars and keep in the fridge.

60ml olive oil
60ml dried crushed chilli
2 garlic cloves
3 ripe tomatoes
1 red pepper
5ml sugar
salt and black pepper
juice of 1 lemon

Crème Caramel

PRE-HEAT the oven to 160°C. Melt the 90g caster sugar and water together in a saucepan until caramel in colour. Pour the liquid sugar into the base of a soufflé dish, rolling it slightly up the side as it sets. Break the egg yolks and eggs into a bowl, add the 30ml of caster sugar and whisk together.

HEAT the milk and orange peel in a saucepan until just boiling. Pour the hot milk over the egg mixture and whisk lightly. Sieve the egg custard into a bowl and pour into the soufflé dish with the caramel base. Place the dish in a baine-marie of hot water, and cook in the oven for 25–35 minutes. It should be slightly wobbly and just set. Remove from the oven and allow to cool. Slip a palette knife around the edge of the crème caramel and turn out onto a large plate.

90g caster sugar
20ml cold water
1 eggs
1 egg yolk
30ml caster sugar
2ml vanilla extract
300ml milk
peel of half an orange

One Night in Bangkok

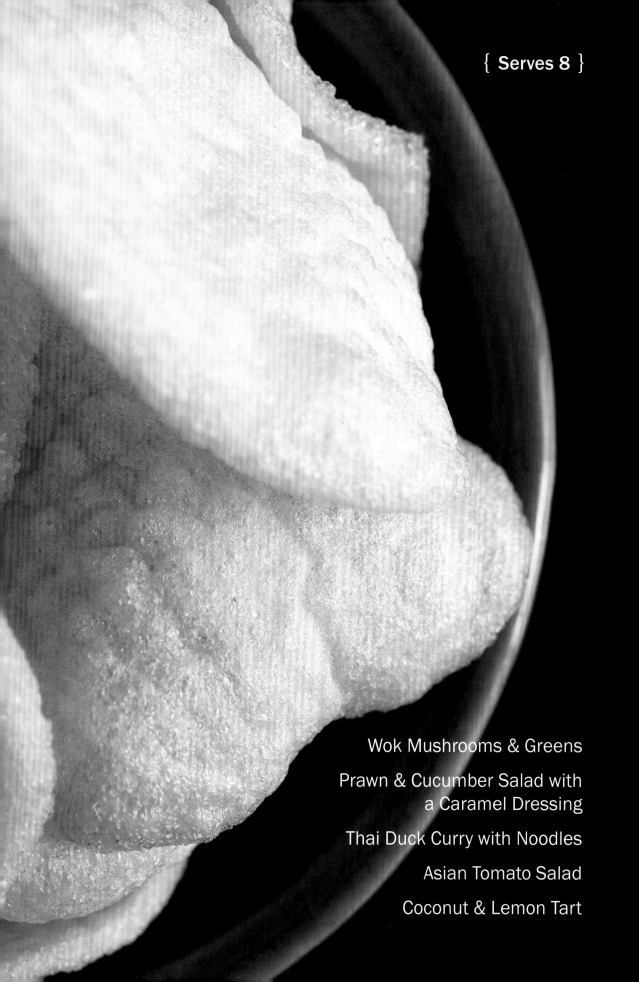

{ Serves 8 }

Wok Mushrooms & Greens

Prawn & Cucumber Salad with
a Caramel Dressing

Thai Duck Curry with Noodles

Asian Tomato Salad

Coconut & Lemon Tart

Wok Mushrooms & Greens

STIR together the soy sauce, corn flour and water, then set aside.

HEAT the peanut oil and sesame oil in a wok and fry the sliced mushrooms for 2 minutes. Season with salt, pepper, crushed garlic, shredded ginger, halved green chillies, half the shredded spring onion and the mange tout.

STIR-FRY for 2 minutes, pour in 150ml of water and bring to the boil. Stir in the corn-flour liquid and oyster sauce. The sauce will thicken. Serve garnished with shredded spring onion.

45ml soy sauce
10ml corn flour
60ml water
30ml peanut oil
10ml sesame oil
125g black mushrooms
salt and black pepper
3 garlic cloves
5cm knob ginger
2 green chillies
bunch spring onions
400g mange tout
15ml oyster sauce

Prawn & Cucumber Salad with a Caramel Dressing

FOR the caramel dressing, pound the garlic, chillies and salt together in a mortar and pestle to make a paste, then stir in 30ml of water and the fish sauce.

MELT the sugar in a saucepan until caramel in colour, then add the garlic paste, garlic oil and lime juice. At this stage be careful as you are dealing with hot sugar. Remove from the heat and stir in the toasted sesame seeds, then set aside.

BLANCH the prawns in salted water for 2 minutes, refresh in iced cold water, drain and tip the prawns in a bowl.

ADD the seeded and thinly sliced cucumber, julienne carrots, shredded lettuce, coriander leaves, mint leaves and shredded spring onion to the prawns. When you are ready to serve, toss the prawns with the dressing, garnish with black sesame seeds and serve.

Caramel Dressing

2 garlic cloves
4 red chillies
5ml salt
30ml fish sauce
30ml caster sugar
15ml garlic olive oil
45ml lime juice
10ml sesame seeds

Salad

16 tiger prawns
1 English cucumber
4 carrots
half an iceberg lettuce
10g coriander
10g mint
10g spring onion
30ml black sesame seeds

Thai Duck Curry with Noodles

PRE-HEAT the oven to 170°C. Season the duck with salt and pepper and fry until browned on both sides. Transfer to a casserole dish. There should be enough fat remaining in the pan from cooking the duck; if not, add some olive oil.

FRY the sliced onion, peeled garlic and shredded ginger until soft, add the crushed cardamom, bruised and chopped lemongrass, saffron, crushed Szechwan peppercorns, coconut milk, water and fish sauce. Cover the casserole with a lid, place in the oven for an hour, remove the lid and bake for another 30 minutes or until the duck is tender and the sauce has thickened and reduced.

HEAT the sunflower oil in a saucepan; when hot, deep-fry the rice noodles. They will puff up immediately; drain on kitchen paper and set aside. Boil the egg noodles in salted boiling water for 5 minutes or until tender, then drain.

DIVIDE the noodles into 8 bowls, top with a duck leg and thigh and spoon over the sauce. Garnish with the deep-fried noodles and coriander leaves.

8 duck leg and thighs
salt and black pepper
3 onions
6 garlic cloves
5cm knob ginger
4 cardamom pods
3 stalks lemongrass
2ml saffron
7ml Szechwan peppercorns
450ml coconut milk
200ml water
50ml fish sauce
50g rice noodles
200ml sunflower oil
2 packets egg noodles

Asian Tomato Salad

MIX the shredded ginger, crushed garlic, sugar, lime zest and juice, fish sauce and soy sauce together until the sugar has dissolved.

TOSS in the quartered tomatoes, finely sliced red onion, seeded and chopped chillies and chopped coriander.

SET aside for 30 minutes for the flavours to infuse. When you are ready to serve, add a splash of peanut oil, toasted crushed peanuts and mint leaves.

5cm knob ginger
2 clove garlic
5ml caster sugar
juice of 1 lime
30ml fish sauce
5ml soy sauce
4 green tomatoes
4 red tomatoes
1 red onion
3 green chillies
10g coriander
30ml peanut oil
45ml peanuts
10g mint

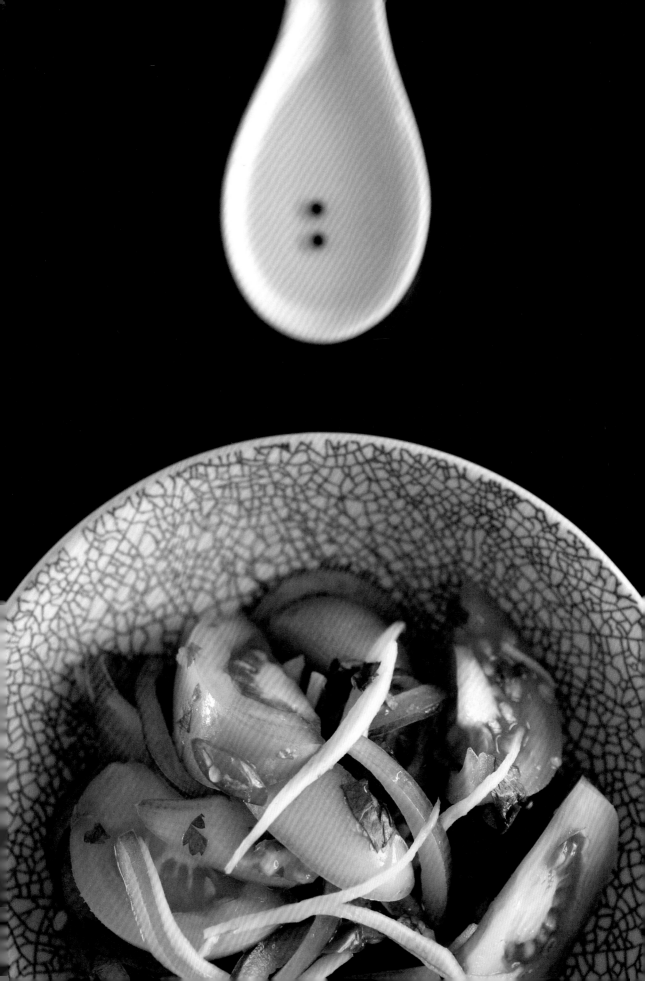

Coconut & Lemon Tart

FOR the pastry, tip the flour, chopped butter, lemon zest and icing sugar into a large mixing bowl. Rub the butter between your fingers until the mixture resembles fine breadcrumbs.

LIGHTLY whisk the egg yolk and milk together, and add three-quarters to the flour mixture. You may not need all the liquid or you may need to add more. Stir until the dough comes together.

TIP the dough onto a lightly floured surface and bring the dough together to form a flattish ball. Wrap in clingfilm and place in the fridge for an hour. Pre-heat the oven to 180°C. Roll out the pastry on a lightly floured surface to line a 24cm tart tin and prick the base of the tart with a fork. Place in the fridge for 10 minutes.

BAKE blind for 15 minutes or until cooked. Meanwhile make the filling, whisk the eggs and sugar together, then lightly whisk in the zest and juice of the lemons, cream and coconut. Scrape the filling into the cooked shell. Bake the tart for 20–30 minutes or until coloured. Cool in the tin for 10 minutes before removing the tart.

Lemon Pastry

250g cake flour
150g butter
zest of 1 lemon
100g icing sugar
1 egg yolk
50–80ml milk

Filling

2 eggs
zest and juice of 2 lemons
200g caster sugar
375ml cream
3 cups desiccated coconut

Vegetarian Buffet

Spinach & Camembert Tart

Asparagus with Sweet Chilli
& Sesame Seeds

Baked Peppers with Cherry Tomatoes
& Blue Cheese

Whipped Bean Purée with Sherry

Honey-roasted Vegetables with Cumin,
Couscous & Feta

Grilled Brinjals with Steamed Eggs

{ Serves 8 }

Spinach & Camembert Tart

PRE-HEAT the oven to 180°C. Roll the pastry to fit a 23cm tart tin and bake blind.

HEAT the oil, chopped red onion and crushed garlic in a saucepan and cook until tender. Add the blanched and chopped spinach, season with salt and pepper, and cook for a couple of minutes, then tip into a bowl.

TIP the spinach mixture into the cooked tart base, crumble over the camembert and gruyère cheese. Whisk the egg yolks, eggs, cream, salt and pepper together and pour over the spinach filling.

BAKE for 20 minutes or until the egg is just set. Cool the tart in the tin for 10 minutes before serving.

250g short crust pastry
15ml olive oil
1 red onion
2 bunch spinach
125g camembert
250ml grated gruyere cheese
2 egg yolks
2 eggs
160ml cream

Asparagus with Sweet Chilli & Sesame Seeds

MIX the water, soy sauce, fish sauce, sesame oil and sweet chilli sauce together and set aside.

HEAT a wok, add the trimmed asparagus and quickly stir-fry for a couple of minutes. Add the shredded ginger and sesame seeds. Once they start to colour, pour in the soy sauce liquid and cook until thick.

ARRANGE the asparagus on a platter and garnish with the coriander leaves.

45ml water
15ml soy sauce
15ml fish sauce
15mls sesame oil
45ml sweet chilli sauce
15ml peanut oil
2 punnets asparagus
5cm knob ginger
45ml sesame seeds
10g coriander leaves

Baked Peppers with Cherry Tomatoes & Blue Cheese

PRE-HEAT the oven to 200°C. Quarter and seed the peppers then lay them skin side down on a baking tray in which the peppers fit snuggly.

PLACE some cherry tomatoes in each quarter, scatter in the sliced garlic, torn basil leaves, salt and pepper and drizzle over the rosemary oil, and roast in the oven for 35 minutes or until the peppers are soft and slightly blackened around the edges. After 20 minutes crumble over the blue cheese.

SERVE the peppers on a platter. Try using feta cheese instead of the blue cheese or adding anchovy fillets. This dish is great served as a starter with crusty bread.

4 red peppers
1 punnet cherry tomatoes
4 garlic cloves
12 basil leaves
12 black olives
salt and black pepper
30ml rosemary olive oil
125g blue cheese

Whipped Bean Purée with Sherry

COVER the beans with water and soak overnight. The following day, drain the beans and set aside.

HEAT the olive oil in saucepan and fry the sliced onion and garlic until soft, add the beans, stirring well to coat them with oil, add water and bring to the boil, simmer for 40–60 minutes, or until the beans are tender.

STRAIN the beans, then tip them into a blender, add the sherry, crushed garlic, salt, pepper, extra virgin olive oil and lemon juice. Blitz to a purée, scrape onto a platter and drizzle with extra olive oil.

150g butter beans
30ml olive oil
1 medium onion
1 clove garlic
45ml sherry
1 very small clove garlic
30ml extra virgin olive oil
juice of half a lemon
salt and black pepper

Honey-roasted Vegetables with Cumin, Couscous & Feta

PRE-HEAT the oven to 200°C. In a mixing bowl, stir together the honey and lemon zest, add the sliced baby marrow (2cm discs) and the chopped brinjals (2cm cubes). Peel the onions and cut into wedges. Seed and slice the peppers. Drizzle with olive oil and season with salt and pepper.

TOSS the vegetables together and tip onto a roasting tray, pour over the vegetable stock and roast for 40–45 minutes or until the vegetables are cooked and the liquid in the tray is thick and caramelised.

PLACE the couscous in a bowl with the cumin, salt and pepper, stir in the hot vegetable stock and set aside for 5 minutes before loosening the grains with a fork.

ADD the chopped herbs, roasted vegetables and crumbled feta cheese. Check the seasoning and serve.

Roasted Vegetables

60ml honey
zest of 1 lemon
2 baby marrow
1 brinjal
1 red onion
4 mixed peppers
60ml olive oil
salt and black pepper
250ml vegetable stock

Cumin Couscous

250g couscous
500ml vegetable stock
10g mint
10g Italian parsley
150g Danish feta cheese

Grilled Brinjals with Steamed Eggs

STEAM the eggs for 7–8 minutes in a bamboo steamer, plunge in water to cool. Carefully peel the eggs and set aside.

GRILL the sliced brinjals in a hot griddle pan until tender. Drizzled with olive oil and season with salt and pepper.

LAY the cooked brinjals onto a platter, top with the quartered eggs, sliced chilli, shredded spring onion and coriander leaves and drizzle over the oyster sauce.

4 eggs
4 brinjals
olive oil
salt and black pepper
2 red chillies
half a bunch spring onions
10g coriander
80ml oyster sauce

Winter Curries

Bombay-style Fish

Spiced Brinjal & Sweet Potato Curry

Tandoori Chicken

Saffron Rice

Gujerati Carrot Salad

Lamb Korma

Spicy Cucumber Wedges

Apple, Peach & Apricot Chutney

Kofta in a Tomato & Yoghurt Sauce

Bombay-style Fish

MIX together the crushed garlic, seeded and chopped chilli, turmeric, cloves, cinnamon, cayenne pepper, tamarind and 100ml of the oil. Place the fish fillets in a shallow dish and spoon the marinade over them. Turn the fish over, cover and refrigerate for 30 minutes.

HEAT the remaining oil in a large, heavy-based frying pan and add the fish in batches. Cook for a minute on each side. Return all the fish to the pan, then reduce the heat to low and add any remaining marinade and the coconut cream. Season with salt and pepper, and cook gently cook for 5–10 minutes, or until the fish is cooked through and flakes easily. If the sauce is too runny, lift out the fish, simmer the sauce for a few minutes, then pour it over the fish. Any fresh fish can be used for this recipe, which is also great with fresh mussels.

GARNISH with chopped coriander leaves and serve with saffron rice, Gujerati carrot salad, spicy cucumber wedges and apple, peach and apricot chutney.

2 garlic cloves
2 green chillies
2.5ml ground turmeric
2.5ml ground cloves
2.5ml ground cinnamon
2.5ml ground cayenne pepper
15ml tamarind purèe
100ml sunflower oil
4 x 180g Cape salmon
1 x 400g tin coconut cream
10g coriander

Spiced Brinjal & Sweet Potato Curry

PEEL off the outer layer of the lemongrass, bruise the base with the back of a knife, then cut off and discard the top half. Put the lemongrass in a food processor with the coriander root and stems, peeled garlic, peeled ginger, chilli, lime leaves and water. Blend for about a minute to a paste.

HEAT the oil in a wok and fry the cubed brinjals in batches until golden brown on all sides, then remove, and set aside. Tip in the sliced onions and cook until soft, add the coriander paste, roasted spice mix, coconut milk, tamarind, fish sauce and sugar. Add the sliced sweet potato. Bring to the boil and simmer for 20 minutes, then add the brinjals and cook for a further 20 minutes or until the sweet potato is tender.

GARNISH with coriander leaves. Serve with saffron rice and spicy cucumber wedges.

2 stalks lemongrass
30ml coriander root and stems
5 garlic cloves
5cm knob ginger
1 red chilli
6 lime leaves
30ml water
60ml sunflower oil
3 red onions
45ml roasted spice mix
600ml coconut milk
30ml tamarind concentrate
45ml fish sauce
30ml palm sugar
500g sweet potatoes
500g brinjals
10g coriander

Tandoori Chicken

PEEL and chop the onion and tip into a blender with the yoghurt, garlic, spice mix, Tandoori paste and oil, and blitz until smooth. Coat the scored chicken with the yoghurt and marinate overnight in the fridge.

PRE-HEAT the oven to 180°C. Heat a grill pan and grill the chicken breast for 5 minutes, season with salt and pepper, turn the chicken over and roast in the oven for 20 minutes or until the chicken is cooked through.

SERVE with a saffron rice, Gujerati carrot salad, and spicy cucumber wedges.

1 small onion
200ml Greek yoghurt
2 garlic cloves
30ml roasted spice mix (page 252)
45ml tandoori spice paste
15ml sunflower oil
4 de-boned & skinned
chicken breasts
salt and black pepper

Saffron Rice

SOAK the rice in water and set aside for 30 minutes. Melt the butter in a saucepan, add the bay leaves and drained rice and cook, stirring, for 6 minutes or until all the moisture has evaporated.

POUR the boiling water over the saffron and pour into the rice, season with salt and pepper. Bring to the boil, cover the saucepan with a lid and simmer for 15 minutes, or until the rice is cooked. Remove the saucepan from the heat and set aside for 10 minutes.

200g basmati rice
15g butter
2 bay leaves
1ml saffron threads
250ml boiling vegetable stock

Gujerati Carrot Salad

HEAT the oil in a frying pan, add the mustard seeds, and once they start to pop, add the julienne carrots. Remove the pan from the heat and season with salt, pepper and lemon juice.

30ml sunflower oil
15ml whole black mustard seeds
3 carrots
salt and black pepper
10ml fresh lemon juice

Lamb Korma

TIP the cubed lamb into a bowl and set side. In a blender blitz the chopped onion, grated ginger, peeled garlic, coriander, cumin, cardamom, cayenne pepper and salt to a smooth paste.

ADD the spice mixture to the lamb with the broken cinnamon and mix well to coat, then marinate for an hour. Heat the oil in a large pan, add the extra sliced onion and cook until soft. Add the lamb in batches and cook, stirring constantly, for 8 minutes until the lamb changes colour. Return all the lamb to the pan and stir in the yoghurt, cream, ground almonds, salt and pepper.

SIMMER for an hour to an hour and a half, or until the meat is tender. Add a little water if the mixture becomes too dry. Check the seasoning and garnish the korma with toasted almonds and coriander leaves.

SERVE with saffron rice, Gujerati carrot salad, and apple, peach and apricot chutney.

1kg de-boned lamb cubes
1 onion
5cm knob ginger
3 garlic cloves
10ml ground coriander
10ml ground cumin
5ml cardamom seeds
large pinch cayenne pepper
1 cinnamon stick
30ml peanut oil
1 onion
125g Greek yoghurt
125g cream
50g ground almonds
flaked almonds
coriander leaves

Spicy Cucumber Wedges

SEED the cucumber, and cut wedges on the angle, tip onto a serving bowl and sprinkle over salt, pepper, cayenne pepper and onion seeds.

half an English cucumber
salt and black pepper
2ml cayenne pepper
5ml black onion seeds

Apple, Peach & Apricot Chutney

IN a saucepan combine the peeled and chopped apples, chopped apricots, sultanas, crushed garlic, chopped ginger, vinegar, sugar, salt and cayenne pepper.

BRING to the boil and cook on medium heat for 30–45 minutes or until you have a thick, jam-like consistency. Stir frequently as it will start to stick to the pan.

POUR into clean, sterilised jars and store in a cool place.

500g Granny Smith apples
110g dried apricots
50g sultanas
6 garlic cloves
2 x 5cm knobs ginger
400ml white wine vinegar
385g caster sugar
10ml salt
2.5ml cayenne pepper

{ Makes 750ml }

Roasted Spice Mix

DRY-ROAST the broken cinnamon in a frying pan with the coriander seeds, cumin seeds, fennel seeds, mustard seeds, fenugreek seeds, crushed cardamom pods, broken star anise and dried chilli until fragrant.

COOL the spices and grind in a mortar and pestle or use a coffee grinder. Be careful not to burn the spices, as this would give a bitter taste.

STORE in an airtight container until ready to use. The spice mix is great used as a marinade for chicken pieces, lamb chops and roasted brinjals.

2 cinnamon sticks
50g coriander seeds
50g cumin seeds
30g fennel seeds
30g mustard seeds
50g fenugreek seeds
5 cardamom pods
3 star anise
1 red chilli

Kofta in a Tomato & Yoghurt Sauce

TO make the kofta, put the grated onion in a sieve and use a spoon to press out as much of the liquid as possible. Tip it into a bowl and mix in the lamb, grated ginger, chopped garlic, seeded and chopped chilli, salt, pepper and egg.

DIVIDE into 16 equal portions and shape each into a ball. Cover with clingfilm and place in the fridge.

HEAT the oil in a heavy-based frying pan over low heat. Add the coriander, cumin, cinnamon stick, ground cloves, crushed cardamom pods and chopped onion, and fry until the onion is soft. Add the turmeric, paprika, garam masala, tinned tomatoes, yoghurt, salt and pepper. Bring to the boil, slide in the chilled meatballs and simmer, uncovered, for 45 minutes or until the meatballs are cooked and the sauce has thickened.

GARNISH with coriander and serve. Serve with saffron rice, Gujerati carrot salad, spicy cucumber wedges, and apple, peach and apricot chutney.

Koftas

1 onion
500g minced lamb
5cm knob ginger
3 garlic cloves
2 green chillies
salt and black pepper
1 egg

Tomato & Yoghurt Sauce

45ml oil
15ml ground coriander
10ml ground cumin
1 stick cinnamon
4 cloves
4 cardamom pods
1 onion
2.5ml ground turmeric
5ml paprika
5ml garam masala
400g can chopped tomatoes
150ml Greek yoghurt
10g coriander leaves

{ Index }

Poultry

BBQ Quail with Sweet & Sour Syrup   102

Chicken Flattie   224

Chicken Meatballs in a Saffron Almond Sauce   102

Chicken Tonnato   64

Herb-roasted Chicken Breast Salad   114

Moroccan Chicken served with Moroccan
    Tomato Sauce   124

Pot Roast Spiced Chicken   214

Tandoori Chicken   246

Thai Duck Curry with Noodles   229

White Cooked Chicken   160

Seafood/Fish

Bombay-style Fish   244

Calamari, Roast Butternut & Chilli Salad   190

Chinese Fried Rice with Prawns   160

Pickled Cucumber with Steamed Trout   114

Potted Smoked Fish with Sourdough Bread   30

Prawns with Chorizo, White Wine & Peas   222

Stuffed Calamari with Dukkah   130

Vegetarian

Beetroot Mousse with Lentil Vinaigrette   180

Butternut & Spinach Gratin with Ricotta Custard   168

Cream Cheese, Carrot & Truffle Tartlets   180

Creamy Sweet Potato, Caper & Spring Onion Salad   92

Crunchy Vegetables with Ricotta Dip   52

Crustless Potato & Green Bean Tart   69

Egg-fried Brinjal with Ginger, Chilli & Mint   76

Grilled Baby Vegetables with Pesto   184

Honey-roasted Vegetables with Cumin,
    Couscous & Feta   240

Mushroom & Almond Pâté en Croute with
    Cranberry & Orange Sauce   184

Mushroom & Tofu Stir Fry   158

Paprika-spiced Potato Wedges   90

Spaghetti Salad with Fried Eggs & Chilli   64

Split Pea Cakes with Cherry Tomato & Sunflower
    Seed Salad   122

Spiced Brinjal & Sweet Potato Curry   244

Spiced Brinjal Burger   86

Spinach & Camembert Tart   236

Tomato Stuffed with Tuna, Garlic & Parsley   100

Accompaniments

Salads

Asian Tomato Salad   229

Avocado Salad with Almond Taratar   104

Calamari, Roast Butternut & Chilli Salad   190

Carrot, Mustard Seed & Feta Salad   116

Cherry Tomato, Potato & Olive Salad   116

Chopped Olive Salad   53

Creamy Sweet Potato, Caper & Spring Onion Salad   92

Green Salad with a Dijon Vinaigrette   69

Gujerati Carrot Salad   246

Herb-roasted Chicken Breast Salad   114

Orange & Cucumber Salad with Orange
    Blossom Water   130

Prawn & Cucumber Salad with a Caramel
    Dressing   228

Quinoa, Rocket, Olive & Tomato Salad with Chopped
    Egg Dressing 190

Red Pepper, Roasted Onion & Thyme Salad 80

Rice, Prawn & Lemon Salad 207

Roasted Beetroot Salad with Lentil Dressing 116

Roasted Cumin Seed & Orange Olives 166

Roasted Pumpkin, Dried Oregano & Bean Salad 132

Simple Greek Salad 108

Spaghetti Salad with Fried Eggs & Chilli 64

Spicy Cucumber Wedges 247

Sweet & Sour Coleslaw 92

Sweet Potato, Pea, Asparagus & Almond Salad 122

Yoghurt Salad with Grapes, Walnuts & Cucumber 82

Sauces/Dips

Almond Taratar 104

Apple, Peach & Apricot Chutney 247

Avocado & Tahini Dip 130

Caper Sauce 68

Caper Vinaigrette 207

Caramel Dressing 228

Chilli Jam 138

Cranberry & Orange Sauce 184

Date, Pear & Red Pepper Chutney 26

Dijon Vinaigrette 69

Egg Dressing 190

Fresh Chicken Stock 176

Garlic Aioli 90

Ginger, Chilli & Mint Dressing 76

Gorgonzola, Raisin & Pine Nut Relish 166

Green Peppercorn Béarnaise Sauce 192

Lentil Dressing 116

Lentil Vinaigrette 180

Mild Chilli Tomato Sauce 30

Moroccan Tomato Sauce 124

Paprika Dukkah 52

Peanut Sauce 138

Peri-Peri Style Sauce 224

Ricotta Dip 52

Roasted Chilli Sauce 200

Roasted Red Pepper Hummus 56

Roasted Spice Mix 250

Saffron Almond Sauce 102

Salsa Verde 40

Smoked Mackerel Dip 108

Sweet & Sour Syrup 102

Thai Curry Powder 140

Tomato & Almond Preserve 174

Tomato & Yoghurt Sauce 250

Tomato Relish 90

Tzatziki 110

Whipped Bean Purée with Sherry 238

Vegetables

Asparagus with Sweet Chilli & Sesame Seeds 236

Baked Peppers with Cherry Tomatoes
    & Blue Cheese 238

Beetroot Mousse with Lentil Vinaigrette 180

Bok Choy, Asparagus & Mange Tout 158

Braised Red Cabbage with Green Fig Preserve 208

Brinjal & Mozzarella Rolls 176

Brussel Sprouts with Caper Vinaigrette
    & Feta Cheese 207

Bulgar-stuffed Baby Marrow 192

Caramalised Onions 40

Carrots with Honey, Ginger & Thyme 194

Coconut Rice 140

Crunchy Vegetables with Ricotta Dip 52

Crushed Potatoes with White Wine, Cherry
    Tomatoes & Herbs 186

Crustless Potato & Green Bean Tart 69

Cucumber Relish with Toasted Rice 142

Cumin Roast Peppers, Tomatoes & Olives 216

Gratin of Mushrooms with Bacon 68

Grilled Baby Vegetables with Pesto 184

Grilled Brinjals with Steamed Eggs 240

Honey-roasted Vegetables with Cumin,
    Couscous & Feta 240

Paprika-spiced Potato Wedges 90

Pesto Dumplings   168

Pickled Spiced Beetroot   176

Poor Man's Potatoes   222

Potatoes with Black Vinegar   158

Pumpkin & Spinach Gratin with Ricotta Custard   168

Roasted Cumin Seed & Orange Olives   166

Roasted Potatoes with Milk, Rosemary & Garlic   214

Saffron Rice   246

Salted-Pickled Cucumbers   86

Spicy Cucumber Wedges   247

Stir-fried Green Beans & Sesame Seeds   142

Sweet & Sour Chickpeas   124

Sweetcorn Cakes   198

Szechwan Brinjals with Water Chestnuts   207

Wok Mushrooms & Greens   228

Zucchini Fritters   110

Desserts

Apple, Raisin & Cream Cheese Cake   149

Banana & Chilli Tatin   170

Benedict Bars   146

Berry & Cream Cheese Tartlets   194

Blueberry Cream Cake   118

Chestnut & Cinnamon Cake with Roasted Plums   110

Chocolate Pecan Nut Cake   148

Chocolate-stuffed Prune & Almond Tart   82

Coconut & Lemon Tart   232

Cream Cheese, Carrot & Truffle Tartlets   180

Crème Caramel   224

Crimson Raisin & Walnut Cake   186

Exotic Fruit Salad with a Raspberry & Lemongrass Sorbet   126

Flourless Chocolate Tart with Poached Pears   72

Fresh Fruit Salad with Lemongrass & Mint   44

Fresh Fruit with Orange Blossom Syrup & Cinnamon Labne   56

Ginger Cheesecake   149

Mango Galettes   16

Maple Pecan Pie with Vanilla Ice Cream   94

Mint Ice Cream with Ginger Biscuits   142

Plum & Custard Tartlets   48

Raspberry & Lemon Grass Sorbet   126

Raspberry Rice Pudding   200

Spiced Peaches   162

Sweet Buñuelos with Orange Curd   104

Syrupy Orange Cake with Ganache 148

Vanilla Custard & Pine Nut Tart   216

Vanilla Ice Cream   94

Vanilla Sponge Cake with Strawberries   146

Vanilla Yoghurt Panacotta with Honey-poached Strawberries   134

Walnut Tart   150

Baking

Almond Lemon Scones   44

Benedict Bars   146

Blueberry Muffins   45

Brinjal & Mozzarella Rolls   45

Carrot, Oat & Pecan Muffins   23

Cheddar, Paprika & Mushroom Muffins   22

Chocolate Pecan Nut Cake   148

Cinnamon & Chocolate Brioche   18

Crimson Raisin & Walnut Cake   186

Herbed Focaccia   76

Honey, Raisin & Almond Cake   32

Morrocan Flat Breads   100

Orange, Fennel Seed & Almond Biscuits   162

Pita Breads   53

Polenta Bread   222

Pot Bread   40

Quick & Easy Dinner Rolls   212

Syrupy Orange Cake with Ganache   148

Vanilla Sponge Cake with Strawberries   146

Beverages

Beetroot, Carrot, Grape & Ginger Juice   48

Café Mocha   22

Homemade Chai Tea   38

Pineapple & Ginger Punch   30

Tropical Juice   22